Scarecrow Studies in Young Adult Literature
Series Editor: Patty Campbell

Scarecrow Studies in Young Adult Literature is intended to continue the body of critical writing established in Twayne's Young Adult Authors Series and to expand it beyond single-author studies to explorations of genres, multicultural writing, and controversial issues in young adult (YA) reading. Many of the contributing authors of the series are among the leading scholars and critics of adolescent literature, and some are YA novelists themselves.

The series is shaped by its editor, Patty Campbell, who is a renowned authority in the field, with a thirty-year background as critic, lecturer, librarian, and teacher of YA literature. Patty Campbell was the 2001 winner of the ALAN Award, given by the Assembly on Literature for Adolescents of the National Council of Teachers of English for distinguished contribution to YA literature. In 1989 she was the winner of the American Library Association's Grolier Award for distinguished service to young adults and reading.

LAURIE HALSE ANDERSON

Speaking in Tongues

Wendy J. Glenn

Scarecrow Studies in Young Adult Literature,
No. 36

THE SCARECROW PRESS, INC.
Lanham • Toronto • Plymouth, UK
2010

Published by Scarecrow Press, Inc.
A wholly owned subsidiary of The Rowman & Littlefield Publishing Group, Inc.
4501 Forbes Boulevard, Suite 200, Lanham, Maryland 20706
http://www.scarecrowpress.com

Estover Road, Plymouth PL6 7PY, United Kingdom

British Library Cataloguing in Publication Information Available

Library of Congress Cataloging-in-Publication Data
Glenn, Wendy J., 1970–
   Laurie Halse Anderson : speaking in tongues / Wendy J. Glenn.
       p. cm. — (Scarecrow studies in young adult literature ; no. 36)
   Includes bibliographical references and index.
   ISBN 978-0-8108-7281-3 (hardback : alk. paper) — ISBN 978-0-8108-7282-0 (ebook : alk. paper)
   1. Anderson, Laurie Halse. 2. Authors, American—20th century—Biography.
3. Authors, American—21st century—Biography. 4. Young adult fiction—Authorship. I. Title.
   PS3551.N374443Z68 2010
   813'.54—dc22
   [B]   2009030545

Printed in the United States of America

To Martin,
my most honest critic and my best friend

Contents

Preface

I'M STANDING IN LINE at the 2008 ALAN Workshop waiting for Laurie Halse Anderson to sign two copies of her *Vet Volunteers* chapter book for my young daughters. When her turn arrives, a young woman ahead of me approaches the table and begins to cry. As she quietly shares her sister's emotional response to *Speak*, another of Anderson's titles geared toward adolescent readers, Anderson stands up, extends her arms across the table, and holds the woman in an embrace.

After the exchange, the woman moves on, but Anderson is obviously shaken, genuinely affected by the story she has just heard. She asks me to give her a moment, a brief silence, a chance to close her eyes and breathe deeply before facing the fans that remain, waiting, wishing, wanting to thank Anderson for her stories, her words, her commitment to what's real and often difficult—for both readers and herself as a writer.

Laurie Halse Anderson writes as though inspired, feeling every word, every thought, of every character she creates. She channels the lives of real readers through her imagination and onto the page, enrapturing those who ultimately see themselves, their lives, reflected in her tales.

In her body of work thus far, Anderson has demonstrated the marked capacity for writing diverse texts for multiple audiences in varying genres, breaking barriers with each title she creates. A unifying thread, however, runs through these works: respect for her readers. Whether she sets out to educate the next generation of Americans about their shared democratic heritage or tell the stories of teens whose voices are often silenced out of fear, misunderstanding, or oppression by adults, Anderson is inspiring and inspired.

In the tradition of the Scarecrow Studies in Young Adult Literature series, this book takes the form of a critical literary biography. It draws extensively from both primary and secondary sources in the attempt to capture a vivid written portrait of Anderson and her works. Any unsourced quotations resulted from a telephone interview conducted by the author with Laurie Halse Anderson in July 2009.

Acknowledgments

A GENUINE AND HEARTFELT thank you goes out to Laurie Halse Anderson for her willingness to share a bit of her time and self as a participant in this project. It has been an honor indeed.

Thanks, too, to the staff at the Homer Babbidge Library on the Storrs campus of the University of Connecticut for help in securing those less accessible source materials.

I utter a proud shout-out to my Husky students (current and former), whose dedication to kids is inspiring. You do great work in this world.

And I owe a very special thank you to Patty Campbell for her keen eye, keener wit, and passion for teens and the literature they deserve.

Chapter One

The Person

LAURIE HALSE ANDERSON's path to writing for young adult readers was indirect, unintentional, and difficult. But the journey along that path—with its protruding rocks, stubborn roots, and occasional perspective-altering twists and views—made her the author she is today. She never set out to write for teens, having detested the adolescent experience when she went through it herself. She had no intention of revisiting those years and, in fact, actively avoided memories of her life as a teen until she was much older.[1]

It was these painful experiences, however, that prepared Anderson to write so effectively for the adolescent audience she now targets, young people who struggle with issues of identity, independence, and choosing right when wrong is sometimes significantly more appealing and easy. Due to her own difficulties as an adolescent, Anderson is empathetic to teens. She describes herself as a "mother/father confessor for this generation,"[2] an adult whom young people trust to listen, hold, and honor their stories with care and dignity and grace.

Anderson possesses great respect for teens, again in large part due to the resiliency she, as a result of her own past, knows they must demonstrate in order to grow into their future. When Anderson speaks of teens, she calls them "the brave ones. They're accumulating scars, but the life hasn't been beat out of them yet."[3] She recognizes the progression adolescents undergo in the pursuit of self:

> I see children as blank sheets of paper. I see teenagers as rough drafts.
> They're always adding details to fit these new personalities. They're

1

putting in new information; they're expanding to fit their larger bodies and their larger sense of self. They cut, they contract, they pull back in when they run up against unexpected pain or harshness; they're always polishing these new versions of themselves, trying to see who will stay in control.[4]

And she clings to the hope that they'll make it out all right, that they'll emerge from this metamorphic experience as stronger—and kinder—people.

Anderson's commitment to creating stories that enrich, disquiet, and guide the teens she admires led to her selection as the 2009 recipient of the prestigious Margaret A. Edwards Award. Committee members describe Anderson's first three novels, *Speak, Fever 1793,* and *Catalyst,* as "gripping and exceptionally well-written," noting how Anderson uses "various settings, time periods, and circumstances" to "poignantly reflect the growing and changing realities facing teens." "Iconic and classic in her storytelling and character development," they argue, "Anderson has created for teens a body of work that continues to be widely read and cherished by a diverse audience."[5] Edwards Committee Chair David Mowery substantiates this view when he says, "Laurie Halse Anderson masterfully gives voice to teen characters undergoing transformations in their lives through their honesty and perseverance while finding the courage to be true to themselves."[6]

Anderson has published four additional novels, *Prom, Twisted, Chains,* and *Wintergirls,* along with several titles for younger readers who'll eventually step onto the road toward teendom. A "hard-headed farmer of books," she continues to explore new territory as she journeys, clearing new paths in the process of culling stories in the way her ancestors, "rock-farming Yankees from the North Country," culled stones.[7]

A HAPPY CHILDHOOD

Anderson was born as Laurie Beth Halse in Potsdam, New York, on 23 October 1961. She is the daughter of Reverend Frank Halse and Joyce Holcomb Halse and the older sister of Lisa.

Anderson describes her pre-adolescent years as "idyllic."[8] Her father, a Methodist minister, worked at a few country churches before becoming a chaplain at Syracuse University when Anderson was in first grade. College students were regular visitors to the house and served as pseudo older siblings to Anderson and her sister. Anderson recalls the simple joys of this time in her life: "My dad was the big man on campus, my mom had a job she loved, and I could walk to school."[9] Anderson describes her father as a "very gifted preacher." As a kid, she says, "I knew that Jesus wasn't really my dad's brother or anything, but I did think he might be, you know, his second cousin or something. But my mother on the other hand had no religion at all. (She married him because he was hot, and tall)."[10]

Anderson grew up connected to the natural world, spending ample time outdoors and with her beloved pets. Her grandfather was a forest ranger, and her dad took her hiking in the Adirondack Mountains with regularity.[11] She was "very fond of salamanders and strange fungal growths that grew on trees."[12] Animals—found in the woods and on her porch—taught her to love and care for something other than herself.[13] They inspired her as a writer, too; the first poem she ever wrote was about her kitten, Soot.[14]

Her writing education was fostered, too, by the stories she heard the grownups telling when she sneaked downstairs after being tucked into bed. In the process of listening, she gained knowledge of pacing, hooks, and dialogue that would fuel her later development as an author.[15] Anderson's early school experiences also fostered this writing identity. She recalls that moment when she realized she had words of her own to share. When her second grade teacher taught her and her classmates to write haiku, Anderson thought to herself for the first time, "Oh, my goodness. I can do this!"[16]

Anderson's childhood was also filled with reading-rich experiences. Although her home contained few books, most of which were religious texts that belonged to her father, she found access to a broad range of written stories in the home of her Aunt Janet, a stern and independent woman whose house, though modest, contained shelves and shelves of titles. Aunt Janet taught Anderson that "books were good and important and worth dedicating part of your life to."[17] This passion was reinforced by Anderson's initial visit to the main branch of the Syracuse Library to get her library card. She remembers, "It was filled with balconies and wrought iron railings—it seemed magical and scary and thrilling."[18] She remembers, too, being surrounded by books in her local school; the elementary school library "was a sanctuary, and it was always warm."[19] Books, wherever found, she recalls, "took me everywhere—ripping through time barriers, across cultures."[20]

FAMILY STRUGGLE

A perceptible shift occurs, however, when Anderson remembers her life as an adolescent. Seventh grade, she recalls, wasn't too bad. Although she is certain the typical teen drama was unfolding all around her, she reports being relatively oblivious. "I remember feeling tall and awkward," she says. "I remember my art class, the gospel choir, and, vaguely, Social Studies. I remember being in a couple of fights and burning my arm on the radiator in the cafeteria. And I remember the long walk there in the winter darkness. Nothing horrible, nothing earth-shattering."[21] Memories of the next few years, however, are filled with family anguish. Anderson explains that she is "actually a very happy person in real life, but I was not a happy teenager. I struggled with depression."[22]

As Anderson describes it, "My father had a falling out, a bloody falling out over a very significant issue with his church, and he left his job, which for my father was a recipe for spiritual suicide."[23] He worked with students in the late 1960s when there was much campus unrest in the United States in response to the Vietnam War. As Anderson explains, "The church thought that type of ministry should go one direction, and my father thought that type of ministry should go another direction. And the church won."

Her parents spent the next several years suffering bouts of mental illness and severe alcoholism, frequently leaving Anderson and her sister to fend for themselves.[24] Anderson suffered spiritually, too, feeling compelled to question deeply what was happening and channeling blame—or at least frustration—toward God. She says, "All teenagers have to rebel against their parents, but when your dad is a minister, sometimes, if you have my kind of personality, you feel compelled to rebel against God, too."[25]

This rebellion, albeit challenging, empowered her to think for herself and take a stand against her church. Anderson remembers being in eighth grade and preparing for her confirmation into the Methodist faith. The night before the event, she visited her pastor and said, "OK, you want me to come tomorrow, and you want me to say all this stuff, and join the church. But how can I do that when you guys are treating my father this way?" As Anderson recalls, "For the first time, I spoke up, and he didn't answer me."[26] She chose at that moment not to be confirmed. Anderson later found a means to foster her spirituality by becoming a Quaker. She still struggles with issues of faith but finds value in trying to be the best person she can be, noting, "I'm a bad Quaker. I'm a Quaker with evil tendencies. But I try really hard."[27]

Although Anderson blamed her father for much of her adolescent pain as it was happening, her perception of him and their resulting relationship grew more positive over time. Although she now describes her father as "a great man," she admits that she didn't think this way when she was a teen. Through these difficult years, she says, "He confused me, bewildered me, infuriated me. I am sure I did the same to him. There was love underneath it all, but lots of pain was smothering it."[28] Anderson finds much to admire in her father today. She describes him in glowing terms:

> My father has been a profound influence on my life and on my writing. He is a poet, first and foremost. This means he sees the world through the eyes of a child, and his heart is pure, and his feelings are easily wounded. He is an alchemist who transmutes emotion into words into laughter and tears. He rages against social injustice and corruption and he cheers good intentions. He is a hopeless optimist. He does not suffer fools gladly. He is committed to the life of a Christian seeker. . . . He has never forgotten the lessons of the Great Depression. He gave a poetry reading last month that left the audience in tears. He loves my mother.[29]

HIGH SCHOOL SURVIVAL

As a teen, Anderson didn't have the distance and subsequent perspective to see her family situation as anything other than pain inducing. This was particularly true when, before Anderson's freshman year of high school, the family moved to "a crappy apartment" in an expensive neighborhood outside of Syracuse, forcing Anderson to leave her familiar surroundings and enter a school in which she, in comparison to her classmates, was poor, a tension her protagonist, Melinda, similarly experiences in Anderson's novel *Speak*.

Anderson's pain was compounded when she was sexually assaulted at the age of thirteen. Her new friends in the apartment complex where she and her family lived introduced her to an older guy, a senior in high school, who lived there, too. He liked Anderson; she liked him. Like Melinda in *Speak*, she was hopeful that starting high school with an older boyfriend by her side might help "ease the passage" into a new setting. One afternoon,

Anderson remembers, they were making out in a secluded area of a park near a pretty brook. At the time, Anderson thought, "That's as far as I'm going to go," but he wanted to have sex. Anderson recalls, "I was so young and sexually naïve, I wasn't even really sure what was happening to me." It was quick, and she went home in shock. She showered until the hot water tank was empty and didn't tell her parents out of fear of adding to the family chaos. She has kept the secret from them since. "The time has long passed for when it would have been appropriate to share that with them," Anderson says. "If I were to tell them it would just be such a burden on their hearts because they would have felt that they should have been there."

Anderson, however, doesn't think that silence is the best response and encourages survivors to speak up. She argues that we have allowed a stigma of shame to be attached to victims of sexual assault, which explains why it so often goes unreported. Victims of other crimes—like robbery or carjacking, for example—don't feel shame in response to their attack and are often afforded extra sympathy and compassion. But in contrast, says Anderson, we too often "demonize the survivors of sexual assault." Anderson is adamant that if more survivors, male and female, would just say "Yup, this happened to me. It sucked. I wish the person could have gone to jail. Let's make sure this doesn't happen again," a currently taboo topic for discussion would be addressed and legitimized.

Anderson found no solace from her familial and personal struggles in high school, which she "endured, not enjoyed."[30] "Frankly," she states, "I hated school." Because she was tall, her teachers asked her to sit in the back row, but when she sat there, she found it difficult to pay attention. As a result, she either "got in lots of trouble" or "ignored the teacher" altogether.[31] Anderson started ninth grade as a member of the Dirt Bag clan, a group of classmates willing to overlook her unfashionable clothes and relative poverty.[32] A voracious reader, she devoured almost every book in the library—but loathed English class. A lover of science fiction and fantasy, in particular, Anderson held J.R.R. Tolkien's *The Hobbit* dear. "I didn't have a closet [like Melinda Sordino]," she argues. "I hid in books."[33] One such book was *Go Ask Alice*, written by an anonymous author whose life spins out of control when she experiments with and eventually becomes addicted to LSD. Anderson found solace, even hope, in this story, realizing that "there was somebody out there whose life sucked worse" than her own.[34]

Given her longtime passion for American history and politics, Anderson found solace, too, in her ninth grade social studies classes. Should writing ever stop making her happy or paying the bills, she would consider a career as an American history teacher.[35] A proud and patriotic American, Anderson is fascinated by the American experiment in democracy.[36] Anderson also holds a continued fascination with foreign cultures and languages,[37] an interest perhaps attributable to her yearnings to escape the agonizing realities of ninth grade.

Tenth and eleventh grade improved slightly. Anderson made two good friends and began dating a nice guy who attended a different high school. These relationships afforded her necessary connection to other young people.[38] She remains in contact with these girlfriends, and although she hasn't seen this former boyfriend in over thirty years, she met his oldest daughter when the girl was a high school student and cast member in a local production of *Fever 1793*. During these years, Anderson was an athlete as well as a writer for the school newspaper and literary journal. Because she participated on the swim and track teams and hung out with the kids in the foreign language wing of the school, she shifted into the Jock and Eurotrash clans. Even so, she remained on the fringe, unable to fully participate. She regrets not trying out for the basketball team or standing up to the girls on the team who wouldn't even look at her despite her height.[39]

In twelfth grade, Anderson escaped.[40] For thirteen months, she traveled to Denmark to work on a pig farm as an American Field Service exchange student. She attended school at Hong Studenter og HF Kursus, worked in the fields, captured runaway ducks, and emerged a different, more resourceful, and content person.

Throughout high school, Anderson kept her personal pain hidden away behind a façade of complacency. In hindsight, she wishes she had communicated what was going on with an adult outside of her family, but at the time, she didn't trust anyone.[41] Although she didn't reach out, some adults did. Anderson attributes her eventual ability to survive these years to the few teachers who held faith and confidence in her. She says:

> I was teetering on the edge of disaster. I was ready to go from soft drugs into very hard and nasty drugs. I was hanging out with people who are all dead now. The reason that I'm not dead is that I had teachers . . . that would look me in the eye and say, "Hi, how are you doing? I haven't

seen you in a while. Welcome back. Now you have to serve detention, but I'll be there."[42]

Although Anderson's family held college expectations for her, she herself wasn't sure she'd make it. Neither were school officials. One guidance counselor told her she was headed for prison.[43] When she did imagine herself as a college graduate, however, she saw herself wearing the white coat of a doctor, an interest still evidenced by the medical references in her *Wild at Heart/Vet Volunteers* series books. She chuckles and admits that her biology teacher may have found this career choice to be plausible, but her chemistry teacher would most surely have laughed.[44]

When Anderson returned home from Denmark, she worked for minimum wage in the stock room of a clothing store, "which quickly convinced her to go to college."[45]

COLLEGE EDUCATION

Anderson worked on a dairy farm while she attended Onondaga County Community College in Syracuse, New York, from 1979 to 1981, graduating with an associate's degree in liberal arts. She calls community college "a godsend."[46] "It had terrific professors, and I could afford it. I did so well there that the nice people at Georgetown University gave me a big honking scholarship. That, combined with a lot of student loans, let me go there."[47] She transferred to Georgetown University in 1981 and received a bachelor's degree in languages and linguistics in 1984. Life at Georgetown was fun but gave her "a totally useless degree and a lot of debt." "I studied historical linguistics," she explains, "which qualifies me to work at the mall."[48] In response to her earlier schooling experiences with teachers who made her analyze books in ways she didn't agree with, Anderson avoided the English Department altogether.[49]

She did, however, hone her math skills by working as a stockbroker for almost a year. During her senior year of college, Anderson was transitioning into the adult world. It was the early 1980s, the Reagan years, and attending business school was all the rage. Anderson had avoided anything to do with math but had friends who were getting jobs as stockbrokers. She assumed that if they could do it, so could she. She earned her license and began work at a local firm in Washington, D.C., cold calling strangers to convince them to invest. According to Anderson, "I was a very bad stockbroker because I was a very good salesperson. I would get people, especially elderly people, who'd go, 'Okay, honey, I have a CD I can cash. Where do I send it?' And then I would talk them out of it. I'd say, 'Oh no, you don't want to do that. This is actually more risky than I first portrayed it, and a CD is a very good place for your money.'" Anderson was soon "encouraged to find a different line of work."

TRANSITION INTO WRITING

A year prior to her graduation from Georgetown, Anderson married Greg Anderson, a computer programmer. In 1985, their first daughter, Stephanie Holcomb, was born. A second daughter, Meredith Lauren, followed in 1987. The family settled in Pennsylvania in 1989. During this time, Anderson was a stay-at-home mom who took creative writing courses to keep her head busy.[50] For years, Anderson enjoyed writing but considered it a hobby more than a career option. When she realized that she might be paid to write, she found work as a freelance reporter—and tried to write adult mysteries in her spare time.[51] This remains her favorite pleasure-reading genre. Anderson simultaneously submitted copies of her completed adult mystery and a picture book manuscript to publishers. She got the picture book contract first, thus setting her on the path to becoming a writer for children and teens.

Her work as a journalist for the *Record* and the *Philadelphia Inquirer* from 1989 to 1992 and as a freelance reporter for various trade journals from 1992 to 1998 allowed Anderson to explore her dual interests in writing and American politics. "When I was a reporter," she remembers, "I spent several fascinating nights at various county headquarters, covering races for president and Congress and school board and dog catcher. When I left the paper, I worked as a campaign volunteer and poll watcher."[52] The greatest benefit of this work, however, resulted from her opportunity to work with editors who, she says, taught her how to write.[53]

During this time, Anderson began her earliest attempts at writing for children. On the day her younger daughter got on the bus and headed to first grade, Anderson sat down to write a book, taking an oath that she would have one published within five years.[54] At first blush, the task proved to be more daunting than she had anticipated. "By lunchtime," says Anderson, "I realized I had no idea what I was doing. I needed help."

To learn more, she traveled to eastern Pennsylvania to attend a one-day conference sponsored by a local chapter of the Society of Children's Book Writers and Illustrators. When she returned home, she "wrote and wrote and wrote," and her manuscripts were "rejected, rejected, rejected." "Clearly," she admits, "I had more to learn."[55] She attended the same regional conference the next year and several years thereafter, finding in the group a supportive community of writers dedicated to crafting meaningful, important stories for kids.

Additional training in writing came through the analysis of the grocery store sacks full of books she checked out from the local library and read to her children. Using the works of these published authors as her guide, she studied the craft of writing on her own, learning what elements might suit and enhance her own style and approach in creating the stories she wanted to tell.[56]

Despite Anderson's commitment to writing as a profession, her mother was skeptical, unconvinced that being a writer was the ideal path for her daughter to pursue. She thought nursing school might be a better option, one that would lead to a degree that would translate into a "real job." It wasn't until she learned years later that Anderson's agent also represents Nora Roberts, her favorite author, that she relented, admitting, "Well, maybe it will work out."[57]

And it did work out, but not without significant work and learning on Anderson's part. Early in her career, she sent off what she describes as several "poorly written books. Great ideas, lousy execution." Each of these manuscripts was rejected, and as Anderson admits, each deserved it. It wasn't until three years and hundreds of rejection letters later that she realized the critical role that revision plays in the writing process. Once she developed the discipline to revisit and reconsider and reconstruct and recraft her stories, the rejection letters transformed into contracts issued by editors who wanted to publish her work.[58]

STORIES TOLD

The tangible results of Anderson's writing education came to fruition in 1996 with the publication of her first picture book for children, *Ndito Runs*. Later that year, Anderson's second picture book, *Turkey Pox*, was released. This was followed in 1998 with the publication of a short story in *Highlights for Children*, a magazine she read and enjoyed as a kid, and a third picture book for children, *No Time for Mother's Day*. During this time, Anderson also wrote nonfiction pieces to supplement her family's income. Her first nonfiction book for children, *Saudi Arabia*, was published in 2000. Anderson also worked as the ghostwriter for psychiatrist Ward K. Swallow in the publication of a nonfiction book for adults, *The Shy Child: Helping Children Triumph over Shyness*, published in 2000.

Anderson enjoyed the time she spent writing for the newspaper but found it depressing sometimes. "Writing for kids," she claims, "was sort of an antidote to that. But then I would get bored because I was only doing picture books in the early days, and they didn't have enough sex and death."[59] It was time to expand her audience.

Anderson began researching, writing, and rewriting the historical young adult title *Fever 1793* in 1993. While she was taking a break from the story of life in disease-plagued Philadelphia, inspiration struck in the voice of Melinda Sordino, and Anderson turned her attention to *Speak*, which was published in 1999. Anderson then finished *Fever 1793*, which was published in 2000. She also began work on the *Wild at Heart* series, originally published by American Girl and later picked up by Penguin and published under the series title *Vet Volunteers*. Another children's picture book, *The Big Cheese of Third Street*, came out in 2001.

Anderson's third young adult novel, *Catalyst*, was published in 2002. *Thank You, Sarah! The Woman Who Saved Thanksgiving*, Anderson's first attempt at creative, historical nonfiction for children, was published that same year.

Anderson's next young adult novel represented a departure from her earlier titles for teens in its comedic elements. *Prom*, "a funny book about a loving family and a girl trying to figure out how to dream big,"[60] was published in 2005. Although she enjoyed the break from immersing herself in the depression and death and sadness experienced by her pre-*Prom* characters, she couldn't ignore the letters from readers, boys in particular, who shared their frustrations about what it means to be a young man in our society. The result, *Twisted*, was published in 2007.

Two titles appeared in 2008. *Chains*, historical fiction for young adults, depicts life in New York City at the start of the Revolutionary War as seen through the eyes of a slave girl. *Independent Dames: What You Never Knew about the Women and Girls of the American Revolution* shares the stories in a picture book format of over eighty women and girls who aided the Patriot cause during the Revolutionary War. Anderson's seventh novel for young adults, *Wintergirls*, was published in 2009. She calls this her darkest novel yet.[61] In contrast, her 2009 picture book *The Hair of Zoe Fleefenbacher Goes to School* provides a lighthearted look at student-teacher cooperation.

LIFE BEYOND WRITING

Although Anderson and her first husband divorced, they remain on good terms. He still checks her manuscripts for grammar errors.[62]

In 2005, Anderson moved from Pennsylvania to Mexico, New York, to be reunited with her childhood sweetheart, Scot Larrabee, a carpenter who built a house on a hill covered with maple trees. "To understand the significance of this," Anderson insists, "you need to know that I fled the region at age 18 at a full gallop. I vowed never, ever, ever, ever to return again. . . . And then God chuckled."[63] Anderson says she fell in love with Larrabee when she was three years old and he was six.[64] Their moms were best friends and drank coffee together during the afternoons. Larrabee was in charge of walking Anderson home from kindergarten. "He taught her how to tie her shoes and whistle. She taught him how to be patient with a girl who always has her nose in a book."[65] Although their moms predicted they'd marry someday, the kids didn't buy it—until their first marriages ended and their paths crossed again after almost twenty years.[66]

Anderson's marriage to Larrabee led to the addition of two stepchildren to her family, Jessica and Christian. Anderson calls this extended, blended family "the greatest thing that has ever happened" to her.[67] She is particularly proud that her family "stands as an example about how to turn a hard thing—divorce and remarriage and all the step-issues—into a fruitful thing."[68] Anderson and Larrabee opened their home to yet another family member in 2005 when they adopted Kezzie, a "slightly neurotic" German Shepherd,[69] who makes a memorable cameo appearance in *Twisted*.

When she's not writing or spending time with family, Anderson enjoys watching college basketball or NFL football, gardening, hiking, or training for various road races. Running has proven especially valuable to Anderson's personal and writing life. She disliked running as a child, due in large part to her asthma, but as an adult, she began running to lessen the stress of being a stay-at-home mom with a toddler, an infant, and little money. Taking a run when her husband returned home from work gave her a means to vent. Now that her kids are grown, Anderson has become more serious about her running, competing in several local races with her husband and finding an invaluable body-mind-soul connection. When she runs regularly, three or four times a week, all facets of her life improve: "My writing goes better, I sleep better, I eat better, and I'm a nicer person. My husband is very supportive of this endeavor."[70]

Given the recent pace of Anderson's publishing record, readers are, too.

NOTES

1. Laurie Halse Anderson, "Loving the Young Adult Reader Even When You Want to Strangle Him (or Her)!" *ALAN Review* 32, no. 2 (2005): 54–55.

2. Anderson, "Loving the Young Adult Reader," 53.

3. Laurie Halse Anderson, "Speaking Truth to Power," speech delivered at the Annual Workshop of the Assembly on Literature for Adolescents, San Antonio, Texas, 15 November 2008.

4. Anderson, "Loving the Young Adult Reader," 55.

5. Macey Morales and Jennifer Petersen, "Laurie Halse Anderson Wins 2009 Edwards Award for Significant and Lasting Contribution to Young Adult Readers for 'Catalyst,' 'Fever 1793,' and 'Speak,'" American Library Association Press Release, 26 January 2009, www.ala.org.

6. Morales and Petersen, "Laurie Halse Anderson Wins 2009 Edwards Award."

7. Julie Prince, "Writing from the Heart: An Interview with Laurie Halse Anderson," *Teacher Librarian* 36, no. 2 (2008): 70.

8. Anderson, "Loving the Young Adult Reader," 54.

9. Anderson, "Loving the Young Adult Reader," 54.

10. Terra Elan McVoy, "Laurie Halse Anderson Meet and Greet," *Terralan*, 22 April 2009, http://terraelan.com.

11. Carol Fitzgerald and Marisa Emralino, "Interview with Laurie Halse Anderson," *Teenreads.com*, August 2005, www.teenreads.com/authors.

12. Kirby Larson, "Laurie Halse Anderson Speaks," 23 March 2009, http://kirbyslane.blogspot.com/2009/03/laurie-halse-anderson-speaks.html.

13. Betty Hicks, "Meet Laurie Halse Anderson," *Children's Literature*, 2000, www.childrenslit.com/childrenslit/mai_anderson_laurie.html.

14. Hicks, "Meet Laurie Halse Anderson."

15. Patricia M. Newman, "Who Wrote That? Featuring Laurie Halse Anderson," *California Kids*, March 2005, www.patriciamnewman.com/anderson.html.

16. "Laurie Halse Anderson," *Authors and Artists for Young Adults*, vol. 39 (Farmington Hills, MI: Gale Group, 2001); reproduced in Biography Resource Center (Farmington Hills, MI: Thomson Gale, 2007).

17. Laurie Halse Anderson, "Live Journal," 24 January 2006, http://halseanderson.livejournal.com.

18. Debbi Michiko Florence, "An Interview with Children's Author Laurie Halse Anderson," www.debbimichikoflorence.com.

19. Florence, "An Interview with Children's Author Laurie Halse Anderson."

20. "Laurie Halse Anderson," *Authors and Artists for Young Adults*.

21. Laurie Halse Anderson, "Live Journal," 30 November 2007, http://halseanderson.livejournal.com.

22. "Dying to Be Thin," *National Public Radio*, 20 March 2009, www.hereandnow.org.

23. Anderson, "Loving the Young Adult Reader," 54.

24. "Q and A with Author Laurie Halse Anderson," *Penguin Group*, 2005, http://us.penguingroup.com.

25. Anderson, "Loving the Young Adult Reader," 54.

26. Anderson, "Loving the Young Adult Reader," 55.

27. Anderson, "Loving the Young Adult Reader," 55.

28. Laurie Halse Anderson, "Live Journal," 3 May 2006, http://halseanderson.livejournal.com.

29. Anderson, "Live Journal," 3 May 2006.

30. Florence, "An Interview with Children's Author Laurie Halse Anderson."

31. Anderson, "Loving the Young Adult Reader," 55.

32. Fitzgerald and Emralino, "Interview with Laurie Halse Anderson."

33. Fitzgerald and Emralino, "Interview with Laurie Halse Anderson."

34. Bill Ott, "A Century of Books: Children's and YA Authors Look Back," *Booklist*, 15 October 2004, 398.

35. Stephanie Holcomb Anderson, "Officially Long Official Biography of Laurie Halse Anderson," *Author Website*, 2008, www.writerlady.com/bioh.html.

36. Kelly R. Fineman, "Laurie Halse Anderson," *Writing and Ruminating: One Children's Writer's Journey*, 19 May 2008, http://kellyrfineman.livejournal.com.

37. Stephanie Holcomb Anderson, "About Me," *Author Website*, 2004, http://www.writerlady.com/me.html.

38. Fitzgerald and Emralino, "Interview with Laurie Halse Anderson."

39. Fitzgerald and Emralino, "Interview with Laurie Halse Anderson."

40. Fitzgerald and Emralino, "Interview with Laurie Halse Anderson."

41. "Exclusive Q&A with Laurie Halse Anderson," *Teen Books (and Beyond!)*, Palatine Public Library, Palatine, Illinois, 17 February 2009, http://palatinelibraryteens.blogspot.com.

42. Anderson, "Loving the Young Adult Reader," 57–58.

43. Florence, "An Interview with Children's Author Laurie Halse Anderson."

44. S. H. Anderson, "About Me."

45. S. H. Anderson, "About Me."

46. Anderson, "Loving the Young Adult Reader," 53.

47. Laurie Halse Anderson, "Live Journal," 9 February 2009, http://halseanderson.livejournal.com.

48. Anderson, "Loving the Young Adult Reader," 54.

49. Newman, "Who Wrote That?"; and Anderson, "Live Journal," 9 February 2009.

50. Christine M. Hill, "Laurie Halse Anderson Speaks: An Interview," *Voice of Youth Advocates* 23, no. 5 (2000): 325–27.

51. S. H. Anderson, "About Me."

52. Laurie Halse Anderson, "Live Journal," 8 November 2006, http://halseanderson.livejournal.com.

53. Anderson, "Loving the Young Adult Reader," 54.

54. Florence, "An Interview with Children's Author Laurie Halse Anderson."

55. Laurie Halse Anderson, "Acceptance Speech for the Golden Kite Award in Fiction," speech presented at the Annual SCBWI Summer Conference, Los Angeles, California, 30 July 2000, http://www.scbwi.org.

56. Newman, "Who Wrote That?"

57. Joan F. Kaywell and Stephen Kaywell, "A Conversation with Laurie Halse Anderson," *Journal of Adolescent and Adult Literacy* 52, no. 1 (2008): 81.

58. "Authors Unleashed: Interview with Laurie Halse Anderson," *TeensRead Too*, 24 January 2009, http://authorsunleashed.blogspot.com.

59. Hill, "Laurie Halse Anderson Speaks."

60. S. H. Anderson, "Officially Long Official Biography of Laurie Halse Anderson."

61. Laurie Halse Anderson, "Live Journal," 5 February 2009, http://halseanderson.livejournal.com.

62. S. H. Anderson, "Officially Long Official Biography of Laurie Halse Anderson."

63. Laurie Halse Anderson, "The Mystery and Magic of Story: A Spell That Connects One Heart to Another," *ALAN Review* 34, no. 1 (2006): 5.

64. "Authors Unleashed: Interview with Laurie Halse Anderson."

65. S. H. Anderson, "Officially Long Official Biography of Laurie Halse Anderson."

66. Laurie Halse Anderson, "Live Journal," 14 February 2006, http://halseanderson.livejournal.com.

67. S. H. Anderson, "About Me."

68. S. H. Anderson, "Officially Long Official Biography of Laurie Halse Anderson."

69. S. H. Anderson, "Officially Long Official Biography of Laurie Halse Anderson."

70. Laura T. Ryan, "Mexico Writer Plots Her Next Challenge: Half-marathon," *Post-Standard*, 10 June 2008, http://blog.syracuse.com/shelflife.

Chapter Two

─────────○─────────

The Writer

A SIGNIFICANT PORTION of Anderson's online journal includes answers to reader questions regarding the writing process, tips for novice authors, and suggestions for breaking into the business. She shares this knowledge not as a means to flaunt her talents and success but to provide aspiring writers with honest advice that demystifies what it means to be an author, advice that often strips away the glamour some mistakenly associate with the profession. She emphasizes the fact that writing is difficult, often lonely work that requires sustained commitment and passion; to be a writer, you have to write—even on those days when the muse appears to be out to lunch. "The conscious, mindful decision to write every day," insists Anderson, "makes me a writer."[1]

REASONS FOR WRITING

Despite the challenges associated with being a writer, Anderson persists. In the process of translating ideas onto paper, she achieves dual goals, one personal and one social. As an individual, Anderson finds solace in the act of writing. "Writing," she says, "saves me over and over again. . . . Writing helps me make sense of things."[2] When she immerses herself in the creation of a story, she channels the "dark, sad, confused, angry bits" of herself into something "constructive and healing."[3] She also wants "to learn, to grow," and so she says, "I try to write about what I don't know, or, if I write about what I know, I push myself to a new level of understanding or a new perspective."[4]

In addition to the emotional benefits she accrues as a result of her writing, Anderson values writing as a means to support the larger community of teen readers willing to listen to what she has to say. The act of reading her writing ideally provides solace for her intended audience, too. "Being a teenager usually sucks," Anderson argues. "It's hard and confusing and few adults have the guts to talk about it honestly. That's my job."[5] Anderson takes this job seriously, refusing to talk down to young people or dismiss their concerns, fears, and frustrations as petty, foolish, or irrelevant. She reads every letter, every e-mail message, every post sent to her by teens from around the world and responds by writing about what these young people express as most important to them—even if their wants take her to places dark and painful.

Sometimes Anderson wishes she could write less weighty books, given the emotional drain that results from spending a year or two immersed in the realities of rape, family dysfunction, academic pressure, and unrealistic body image, among other issues. But then, she reveals, "I get amazing letters from readers who tell me that one of my books helped them get through a tough time, and I know that this is what I am meant to do."[6] When Anderson writes, the line between her experiences and those of her characters blurs; her empathetic nature allows and demands that she feel, as much as possible, what they feel. To survive this process of emotional immersion, Anderson remembers the kids who write to her, reminding herself of "how much more difficult it is for the teen readers who are struggling with these issues in real life. At least I have the option of walking away from the story. They don't."[7]

WRITING ROUTINES

Before beginning her three most recent novels, Anderson visited a truly special chair at the river's end bookstore in Oswego, New York. The tradition began when Anderson moved to Mexico, New York, in 2005. Upon arriving, she went in search of two essentials—a bookstore and a Thai restaurant. She found both in Oswego. Anderson says, "There's a good vibe in the store." So "when it was time to pound out those opening lines" of *Twisted*, *Chains*, and *Wintergirls*, the comfy chair provided a productive place to let the ideas that had long percolated in her mind emerge on paper.

Although she prefers to write at home, Anderson is able to compose wherever she can find a place to flip open her laptop. *Prom* was written in her "home office" on the right-hand side of the couch in the small Philadelphia apartment she shared with her daughter, Meredith.[8] Other titles have been drafted and revised on airplanes and trains during her travels or in hotel rooms when she has, on occasion, holed up for a few weeks to crank out significant numbers of pages in response to a looming deadline.

When Anderson writes at home, her office is situated on the third floor of the house and contains a picture window that faces the surrounding woods and meadows. The loft can become chilly in the winter, however, so the coldest days are spent writing in the living room in front of the fire. Of late, however, Anderson has witnessed the steady construction of a new office—a writing cottage, powered by solar energy, heated by a woodstove, and built around a salvaged, 125-year-old stained-glass window—in the forest beyond the house. Her husband, the carpenter, gently nudged this idea along, arguing that Anderson's existing office space is too cluttered.[9]

Anderson is a creature of habit, a writer who maintains and values a consistent daily routine. She generally wakes up between 5:00 and 6:00 each morning and eats breakfast while checking her e-mail and posting a blog entry on her live journal. She follows this with a sustained block of writing time. She avoids e-mail and the Internet and refuses to answer the phone or incoming instant messages, taking a break only for tea. Following this writing session, she eats lunch and then heads outside for a run or to the gym for a workout. This is followed by dinner and bookkeeping or other office-related tasks. If the television is flipped on, it's set to a channel broadcasting a college basketball or NFL football game, depending on the season, and Anderson cheers and scoffs accordingly while she responds to any lingering e-mail messages. Then she reads until she falls asleep.

Because Anderson holds young adult literature and its authors in high regard, she refuses to read YA titles when she is in the process of crafting one of her own. "Books and characters I love tend to stick around in my head, like ghosts," she says. By not reading other strongly crafted characters, she is able to ensure that, as she says, "the voices of my characters are coming solely from me."[10] Instead, she fills her mind with tidbits of history garnered from nonfiction texts, adult mysteries, and poetry. When the weather cooperates, she might try to squeeze in some time in the garden. Although she doesn't work as much on the weekends as during the week, she commits herself to writing and reading every day of the year.[11]

An iPod aficionado, Anderson listens to music of multiple varieties as she writes—bass-thumping techno and house music to get and keep her going, the more soothing sounds of the Eagles to settle her in, a bit of Coldplay, a classical melody, whatever suits her frame of mind. She also develops a playlist for each novel she writes and makes it available to interested readers via her author Web site. Each playlist features a collection of songs that put her in the right mood while she worked her way through each scene, each chapter.[12]

INSPIRATION

Anderson is committed to writing about issues that she thinks matter, rather than what she or her editor thinks might sell. When pondering issues that she might tackle in her contemporary works for teens, she considers what frustrates her or makes her angry. "Given how poorly teenagers are treated by the culture," she argues, "I have a lot of material to work with."[13] In her historical fiction, she is choosy, recognizing the amount of research required to backfill a story situated in a place and time unfamiliar to readers. Her approach here is to select topics that fascinate her. "If I don't have an overwhelming curiosity about a time period or situation, I won't touch it," she says. "I need to be on fire about something in order to commit to the research and the challenge of writing."[14]

Her ideas for novels typically come at a rapid pace, generally once each day. The idea might be inspired by something she's reading, a random event she witnesses while out running errands, a snippet of conversation that causes her to "ponder the magic words: 'what if . . . '"[15] Anderson's schedule certainly couldn't accommodate the pursuit of all of these ideas, however. Given this limitation, she must make some difficult choices. To determine which ideas to pursue and which to let go, she envisions each story idea as a watermelon seed, one with potential but one that will require ample work and care to nurture into something worth harvesting. To thrive, the seed must be "planted in well-balanced soil with good drainage at the right time of year, properly watered, weeded, and guarded from bugs and critters."[16] Ideas worthy of this investment of care and nurturing are planted.

Anderson draws very little from her own life when determining the stories she'll tell and then bringing them to life. Instead, she looks to the larger community and world to see how things work and then makes up the rest. Where appropriate, she'll pay close attention to the heated argument she witnesses at the coffee shop or listen carefully to the story shared by her daughter or a friend. Then she'll draw from her own imagination to weave and craft the scenes that precede, follow, and shape the real-to-life moments that find their way into the narrative. Anderson, however, doesn't distance herself completely. As a person, as a mother, as a friend, as a girlfriend, she has garnered life experiences that transfer to her storytelling in nonliteral, more emotional ways. As she explains, "I know what it feels like to fall in love, fall out of love, be starry-eyed, have a jealous fit. Whatever the emotional tenor of the scene requires, I've been there. So even if I make up every single detail of the scene, the emotions probably echo something I've lived through."[17]

PROCESS

When Anderson speaks of her writing process, she uses such terms as "muddle" and "messy" and "stumble forward." However, this seeming disarray, when viewed as a broader process, falls into a relatively consistent pattern.

Devising the Early Drafts

Anderson typically begins a new writing project by honing in on a character or moment in history that bothers or interests her. She'll let the idea simmer for a year or more while working on other projects. Before writing even the first word of a new piece, she'll have in mind a sense of the protagonist and envision a few scenes. When the "thoughts and whispers" start to come to her, she'll jot them down until the jottings get longer and longer, and she ends up with a first draft that she calls "a confusing horror."[18] In the creation of this first draft, Anderson isn't so concerned with stylistic elements or even coherence from chapter to chapter. Instead, she strives to get the bare bones on paper. "If I can clearly hear a conversation or see a setting detail or an image," she explains, "I'll stick it in, but I don't agonize about the little stuff when I'm painting with the broad brush."[19]

Anderson uses the early exploratory drafts to get to know her characters and attune herself to the voice of the narrator, as well as determine the plot structure that will ultimately guide each scene. However, if she has an epiphany regarding a scene or chapter that should take place beyond the one she's in the midst of crafting, she'll jump ahead and simply label the skipped section with a general phrase like "Chapter Four: Something happens."[20]

Anderson starts each new work on what she thinks will be the first page. Quite frequently, however, the opening of the published piece is significantly different from what was originally noted on the page. Earlier versions of *Fever 1793* had eight additional chapters preceding the current version of chapter one, and the opening scene of *Twisted* was tweaked considerably over time.[21] Similarly, as the drafts progress, scenes are moved, elaborated on, or thrown out as the narrative takes shape.

Anderson refuses to allow anyone, even her most trusted readers, to see these first drafts, treating them as messy spaces in which she, like a mad scientist, hunches over her workbench, concocting and mixing, creating and destroying, until the work takes a form she can hand over with satisfaction. In her typically humble way, she claims, "I don't know that I am a good writer. I do believe I am a better than average reviser."[22]

Determining Plot Structure

Anderson's approach to plotting varies depending on the kind of book she is writing. In her contemporary fiction, plot typically takes a back seat to character. In these early drafts, she allows her story to "meander around" in the process of learning more about character backgrounds and motivations, even if several of these discovery scenes are eventually cut.[23] Anderson permits herself to "write whatever weirdness pops in [her] head" and then, in later drafts, she will "sort through the chaos and try to give it structure and a sense of flow."[24] She faults some of her early, unpublished writing attempts for being too plot-driven and thus limited. In the process of plotting everything out in "excruciating detail," she felt in control and aware of what was to come in every scene but didn't open herself to the possibility that her characters might tell her what should come instead. In writing *Speak*, she learned that the process of really getting to know the character made for a more compelling story.[25] In her later contemporary novels, she affords herself this same freedom, recognizing that, if she focused solely on plot from the start, "the stories would never go beyond problem novel fare."[26]

Writing historical fiction requires a different, more plot-oriented approach. Anderson outlines the progression of each scene carefully to ensure that the protagonist's journey aligns well with the realities of the time and place in which he or she lives.[27] Although the scenes in these stories are developed more systematically, Anderson keeps tabs on her characters by maintaining a separate journal.[28] Her ultimate goal is to weave these two strands together—"the exterior plot of the story that deals with the historical events and the interior plot arc of [the] main character, which must be woven in with the historical events."[29] Once the first draft is complete, Anderson looks over the novel as a whole, examining how each component thread might work its way through the story from beginning to end. Each of these threads must be evaluated to ensure that "the events that pull it forward unfold in a way that makes sense, both for that thread and for the larger story."[30] To aid her in this process, she often creates a timeline of events on a large sheet of paper, collapsing and expanding scenes as needed.[31]

Creating Characters

The creation of Anderson's characters in any given piece begins months before she sits down to type the first word. She likens the process to creating an imaginary friend: "I figure out what her life is like, what she loves, what she hates, what's going on in her family, etc."[32] Once she begins to write, Anderson puts her protagonist in uncomfortable situations that force the character to respond. Through this process, Anderson is able to identify the conflicts in her character's life—the driving force behind her or his development over the course of the novel. Anderson explains, "If I've developed conflicts that are organic and in keeping with the character's world, her/his response to the conflicts will naturally lead to internal growth."[33]

Sometimes, however, characters aren't invited to stick around, particularly secondary characters that don't prove necessary to the growth of the protagonist. Although it pains Anderson to cut any characters she's grown to know and love in the early process of drafting, sometimes she has to let go. She consoles herself, however, saying, "I can always send her flowers, take her to the movies, or go out for coffee with her. But if she isn't a vital thread in the fabric of the story, out she goes. I think I have to test out my characters, sometimes following them down the wrong path, to get to know them better and to understand the world of the story."[34]

Selecting Point of View

For now, Anderson is content to employ first-person narration in her novels for teens. She believes the introspective nature of the first-person voice suits her readers well. Teenagers, she says, "are intensely aware of their own perspective on things."[35] Stories that use the first-person voice mimic a teen's vision of the world and encourage connection between the reader and the narrator. Earlier drafts of *Speak* and *Fever 1793* were told in third person, but Anderson decided this voice made the story feel "distant and cold."[36] Anderson wants more than connection from her readers, however, and appreciates the way in which first-person narration is unreliable and thus questionable. Anderson strives to hold her teen readers accountable for evaluating both what the narrator says and how the other characters respond to what the narrator says. Her readers "have to make up their minds about what is perspective and what is truth,"[37] much like they have to do in their nonfiction lives.

Anderson strives, too, to create a first-person voice that's authentic even when she knows it can't be fully realistic. She points particularly to the challenge of writing believable teen dialogue when she can't include the profanity that is so often a part of adolescent discourse. She faces this challenge by attempting to "show through action and narrative details the situations of daily high school life that leads teens to curse a lot."[38]

Honing in on Language

It's not until late in the writing process that Anderson concerns herself explicitly with the more formal aspects of writing such as language conventions, figurative language, imagery, and so on. At this stage, she'll "tinker with the finer story threads and language and image systems and consistency issues until the editor finally peels [her] fingers off the manuscript and takes it away to be published."[39]

This is not to say that her earlier drafts don't contain evidence of an author's multiple techniques. Sometimes, however, it's not until the end of a piece that Anderson identifies the existence of an unintended symbol or image or metaphor. She says that symbolism, for example, "often creeps up and takes the author unaware. Sometimes she feels really stupid about the whole thing and does not understand what she's writing. But eventually, it dawns on her. There are words hidden under words hidden under words."[40] Once these poetic words reach up and tweak her nose, she reviews the text to strengthen her psyche's subversive contribution.

Conducting Historical Research

Anderson prides herself on the quality of research conducted in the creation of her historical fiction. Her propensity and passion for historical detail provide both motivation and a commitment to accuracy. For each of her historically situated works, Anderson asked historians with expertise in the time period to review the fictional account for accuracy.[41] Although most of the characters in her historical novels are fictional, she strives to craft them "as true to what people were like back then as possible," and when real people like George Washington find their way into her books, "they only do or say things that [she] can prove they did or said."[42] Occasionally, however, the evidence just can't support the story she wants to tell. After talking with a historian on the telephone and learning that a crucial bit of history that she wanted to incorporate into her draft of *Chains* could not be verified, she was forced to cut out a "favorite section of book due to lack of primary sources."[43]

To educate herself about the necessary historical details that undergird her fiction, Anderson immerses herself in popular books that describe the time period in which the story is set and reads specialized historical journals. Additionally, she is a regular visitor to several history-oriented listservs that provide access to expert knowledge. She supplements this knowledge by delving into collections held by academic libraries and reading the works of expert historians, whose bibliographies provide references to valuable primary source materials, including newspaper accounts, letters, and advertisements.[44]

Given the amount of material she gathers, Anderson is forced to be an expert organizer. "I keep copious notes," she says, "and often have nightmares in which I am drowning in a sea of citations."[45] Anderson chuckles when interviewers ask if she employs a research assistant to ease her burden, citing her limited income and subsequent ability to afford such a helper. More significantly, however, Anderson isn't sure she'd hire someone even if she could. She says, "I have stumbled across so many wonderful tidbits in the course of researching my historical novels, things that have made my books much richer, that I'm glad I have to do my own digging. I would worry that a research assistant wouldn't realize gold if s/he stumbled across it."[46]

Dealing with Distraction and Difficult Days

Every day is not a happy day in the land of literary creation. According to Anderson, "I freak out about my writing ALL THE TIME. As in, every day. Sometimes many times a day. I am a neurotic, self-doubting, insecure bowl of Author-Jello."[47] These feelings of doubt and anxiety manifest themselves in multiple ways. In the midst of writing each of her novels, for example, Anderson stumbled upon a "mirage . . . a better book in the distance," calling to her. "Come to me," a voice teased, "I am the perfect novel. Look—aren't my characters more interesting? Doesn't the plot turn delightfully? You know you want to write me." Although Anderson isn't sure whether this diversionary source resides in "desperation, fear, or inadequacy," she knows she needs to face it—or it lingers. To quiet this voice, she typically takes a few hours away from her current project and jots down the new ideas swirling in her head.[48]

Anderson also turns to other projects when the one she's working on isn't going her way, if only, as she claims, "to fool myself into believing I am making progress."[49] When her writing takes a wrong turn, it's sometimes difficult to know what went wrong, especially when things felt so right as she was drafting. Anderson says, "You get a great plot idea and you get all excited about it and then you write and write and then . . . things . . . slow . . . down . . . and you realize that if your story were a car, you'd be stuck in the middle of nowhere and your gas tank is almost empty and you forgot to charge your cell phone."[50] At these times, busying her mind with other projects allows her to return with more clarity. Anderson has accepted these moments of confusion as part of her process, seeing them for what they are. "Picture a person trying to decorate a room in total darkness," she suggests. "That's what writing feels like to me a lot of the time. I flail around in confusion and doubt, trying to remember where I put everything. I fall down a lot."[51]

Often these false starts and missteps require Anderson to hit the delete key, cutting forty, sixty, eighty pages of writing she has invested time and energy into creating. Even when she knows it's coming, having identified scenes that just aren't working as they should, cutting chunks of the story remains emotionally tough. For Anderson, the process "feels like breaking up with someone that you know in your head you should break up with but your heart keeps reminding you of the 'good days.'"[52] When Anderson first began writing, she was angry and upset when her work ended up on the chopping block, even when it ultimately improved the quality of the piece at hand; it was just too difficult to witness such a waste of time manifested in the pages removed. Now, however, she sees it as both inevitable and necessary in the creation of stories worth reading. After hitting the delete key, she says, "I just mutter a little and get back to work."[53]

Revising, Revising, Revising

Anderson insists that her strength as a writer resides in her ability to revise. The completion of all of her works to date has demanded at least seven drafts beyond the first. Although she wishes she could produce a finished product more quickly, "slow and steady" seems to suit her and her style best.[54] Most of her writing, she claims, occurs in the process of revision; "the significant structural work and character development happen in drafts two through five."[55] Not until she's reached this fifth draft will she share the work with her editor.

Anderson credits her work as a newspaper reporter as the best preparation for the task of writing (and revising) fiction for teens and children. She argues that, in both forums, "you've got a limited space, so you have to search for just the right detail that will help tell your story. And there's no room for fluff."[56]

For Anderson, the last stage of revision proves the most rewarding part of the writing process. During this stage, she immerses herself in the manuscript for extended periods of time, often sequestering herself away from family members and friends for twelve-hour stretches, or even days, by hiding out in a local hotel room. This complete involvement in the story allows her to "hold all of the story threads" in her mind simultaneously, to "remember every obscure fact—and every 'fact' that contradicts it, to find new joy in the contrasting interpretations."[57] More significantly, it allows

Anderson to remember why it was so important for her to write the piece in the first place. As Anderson explains, "When I give a story every waking minute, I fall in love with it all over again."[58]

Anderson says she experienced this need to dive in fully in the final stage of every one of her novels. Her pattern—"work to exhaustion, sleep, eat, work some more, exercise, eat, work to exhaustion, start again the next morning"—gives rise to some of the most memorable scenes in her writing.[59] The scene in *Twisted* involving the gun, for example, was born in such moments.

Garnering Feedback

When she lived in Philadelphia, Anderson belonged for ten years to a writing group consisting of a core group of ten writers for children and young adults. They met each month in the morning at the public library and read portions of their works in progress and received substantive and significant feedback. Anderson misses these exchanges now that she lives in a remote part of New York and is unable to join her old friends. She now turns to a core group of early readers (close friends and oldest daughter) when she seeks eyes other than her own.[60]

THE NONWRITING ELEMENTS OF WRITING

After any one of her works is published, Anderson must deal with the nonwriting endeavors required in her role as a writer. These range from dealing with the judgments of reviewers to going on a book tour to visiting schools and interacting with young people.

Considering Reviewer Response

Anderson reads reviews by professional publishers as well as active bloggers who show an interest in young adult texts. She likens reading a negative review to "dunking your face into a vat of battery acid. Painful and dumb."[61] While reading a positive review, however, might not hurt, it leaves Anderson feeling unsettled. Anderson will usually read any given review once. If she finds something positive, she feels grateful. If she finds something constructively critical, she tries to learn and move forward. For those reviews that make her "sting," however, there is only one remedy—"liberal applications of comfort food. Mashed potatoes work especially well."[62]

Addressing Controversy

Anderson must deal, too, with attempts at censorship directed at her published works, a reality she has faced (to date) following the publication of *Speak*, *Catalyst*, and *Twisted*. Although some readers take offense at the references to sexuality and the language contained in her novels, Anderson says these responses have not affected the way she writes.[63]

She argues further that she doesn't write controversial teen novels. Instead, she writes about "age-appropriate conflict" for her audience.[64] Adult writers can choose any content; writers for children "try to tell difficult stories in a way that will allow the reader to think and mature."[65] Writing for teenagers, however, puts authors "smack in the middle of these two worlds." Anderson argues that teens cannot be protected from reality: "sex, violence, substance abuse, cheating, academic, social and family pressures, confusion—you name it, most of them are dealing with it,"[66] she says. "In my books, characters mess up. They make mistakes. Sometimes they drink. Sometimes they have sex. Sometimes they cut class and are disrespectful to adults. They mess up and then they have to deal with the consequences of messing up—just like in real life. I don't think any of that is controversial. I think my books are honest reflections of adolescent life today."[67]

Going on Tour

Following the publication of a new novel, Anderson goes on the road for weeks at a time to promote the text and interact with readers and fans from around the United States. Anderson is grateful to the publishers who support these jaunts financially and the booksellers who host her. She demonstrates her appreciation by throwing herself into a truly packed schedule while she's away. "Because I value what these folks are doing for me so highly," she explains, "my time and energy while on tour are fully at their disposal." This results in days beginning at 3:30 a.m., frequent flights from one city to the next, days spent signing books and visiting schools, evenings spent speaking at local libraries, and few bedtimes before 10:00 p.m.

Although this demanding daily agenda means she rarely has time to exercise or maintain a consistent writing schedule, both essential to her sanity, she draws energy by interacting with teen readers and their teachers, many of whom travel significant distances to meet her.[68]

Visiting Schools

During the first six years following the publication of *Speak*, Anderson traveled far and wide (even to Warsaw, Poland) speaking to teachers and librarians at professional conferences and spending time with more than 500,000 middle school and high school students during school visits. One year, she traveled for 120 days of the year.[69] In 2007, however, her publishers placed additional demands on her time, asking her to pick up the pace in her writing. As a result, Anderson has limited her number of school visits—although she has recently discovered the potential of online conferencing via Skype, an online service that allows long-distance conversation using a Web camera. This technological medium might allow her to visit schools in a virtual way, a more workable alternative to physically being present.

IT GOES ON AND ON AND ON

Anderson is regularly in the process of creating multiple products. She typically has one book in the research phase, another in early draft form, another in revision, and yet another close to publication. "Bored Laurie is not a pretty sight," she explains. "Think thunderclouds. Big thunderclouds swirling into funnels."[70] For Anderson, writing keeps the storms at bay.

NOTES

1. "Laurie Halse Anderson Chats with Readergirlz," *Readergirlz*, 23 June 2008, wwwmitaliblog.com/search/label/Author%20Interviews.
2. Carol Fitzgerald and Marisa Emralino, "Interview with Laurie Halse Anderson," *Teenreads.com*, August 2005, www.teenreads.com/authors.
3. Laurie Halse Anderson, "Frequently Asked Questions," *Author Website*, www.writerlady.com/faqh.html.

4. Kirby Larson, "Laurie Halse Anderson Speaks," 23 March 2009, http://kirbyslane.blogspot.com/2009/03/laurie-halse-anderson-speaks.html.

5. Fitzgerald and Emralino, "Interview with Laurie Halse Anderson."

6. Julie Prince, "Writing from the Heart: An Interview with Laurie Halse Anderson," *Teacher Librarian* 36, no. 2 (2008): 70.

7. "Let's Welcome Laurie Halse Anderson to The Family Room!" *Barnes and Noble Online Bookclub*, 30 June–4 July 2008, http://bookclubs.barnesandnoble.com/bn/board.

8. Laura T. Ryan, "More from Laurie Halse Anderson," *Post-Standard*, 22 April 2007, http://blog.syracuse.com/shelflife.

9. Laurie Halse Anderson, "Live Journal," 3 March 2009, http://halseanderson.livejournal.com.

10. Laurie Halse Anderson, "Live Journal," 26 October 2005, http://halseanderson.livejournal.com.

11. Anderson, "Frequently Asked Questions."

12. Anderson, "Frequently Asked Questions."

13. "Q and A with Laurie Halse Anderson," *YAthenaeum*, 6 January 2009, http://yathenaeum.blogspot.com.

14. Kelly R. Fineman, "Laurie Halse Anderson," *Writing and Ruminating: One Children's Writer's Journey*, 19 May 2008, http://kellyrfineman.livejournal.com.

15. Laurie Halse Anderson, "Live Journal," 7 March 2006, http://halseanderson.livejournal.com.

16. Anderson, "Live Journal," 7 March 2006.

17. Laurie Halse Anderson, "Live Journal," 7 December 2006, http://halseanderson.livejournal.com.

18. Joan F. Kaywell and Stephen Kaywell, "A Conversation with Laurie Halse Anderson," *Journal of Adolescent and Adult Literacy* 52, no. 1 (2008): 81.

19. Laurie Halse Anderson, "Live Journal," 15 July 2005, http://halseanderson.livejournal.com.

20. Laurie Halse Anderson, "Live Journal," 8 March 2006, http://halseanderson.livejournal.com.

21. Anderson, "Live Journal," 8 March 2006.

22. Laurie Halse Anderson, "Live Journal," 10 September 2007, http://halseanderson.livejournal.com.

23. Anderson, "Frequently Asked Questions."

24. Anderson, "Frequently Asked Questions."

25. Christine M. Hill, "Laurie Halse Anderson Speaks: An Interview," *Voice of Youth Advocates* 23, no. 5 (2000): 326.

26. Laurie Halse Anderson, "Live Journal," 16 February 2009, http://halseanderson.livejournal.com.

27. Anderson, "Frequently Asked Questions."

28. Anderson, "Frequently Asked Questions."

29. Laurie Halse Anderson, "Live Journal," 9 January 2009, http://halseanderson.livejournal.com.

30. Laurie Halse Anderson, "Live Journal," 10 March 2008, http://halseanderson.livejournal.com.

31. Anderson, "Live Journal," 10 Mar. 2008.

32. Laurie Halse Anderson, "Live Journal," 25 July 2005, http://halseanderson.livejournal.com.

33. Anderson, "Live Journal," 10 March 2008.

34. Laurie Halse Anderson, "Live Journal," 20 February 2008, http://halseanderson.livejournal.com.

35. Holly Atkins, "An Interview with Laurie Halse Anderson," *St. Petersburg Times: Tampa Bay*, 15 December 2003, www.sptimes.com,.

36. "Let's Welcome Laurie Halse Anderson to The Family Room!"

37. Hill, "Laurie Halse Anderson Speaks: An Interview," 326.

38. James Blasingame, "Interview with Laurie Halse Anderson," *Journal of Adolescent and Adult Literacy* 49, no. 1 (2005): 72.

39. Kaywell and Kaywell, "A Conversation with Laurie Halse Anderson," 81.

40. Laurie Halse Anderson, "Speaking Out," *ALAN Review* 27, no. 3 (2000): 26.

41. Fineman, "Laurie Halse Anderson."

42. Fineman, "Laurie Halse Anderson."

43. Laurie Halse Anderson, "Live Journal," 25 February 2005, http://halseanderson.livejournal.com.

44. Fineman, "Laurie Halse Anderson." See also Linda M. Castellitto, "Making History Come Alive for Young Readers," *First Person Book Page*, November 2008, www.bookpage.com.

45. Fineman, "Laurie Halse Anderson."

46. Prince, "Writing from the Heart," 70.

47. Anderson, "Live Journal," 16 February 2009.

48. Laurie Halse Anderson, "Live Journal," 21 June 2005, http://halseanderson.livejournal.com.

49. Laurie Halse Anderson, "Live Journal," 21 July 2005, http://halseanderson.livejournal.com.

50. Anderson, "Live Journal," 21 July 2005.

51. Anderson, "Live Journal," 7 March 2006.

52. Laurie Halse Anderson, "Live Journal," 26 August 2005, http://halseanderson.livejournal.com.

53. Laurie Halse Anderson, "Live Journal," 15 January 2008, http://halseanderson.livejournal.com.

54. Laurie Halse Anderson, "Live Journal," 16 December 2005, http://halseanderson.livejournal.com.

55. Kaywell and Kaywell, "A Conversation with Laurie Halse Anderson," 81.

56. Laura T. Ryan, "More about *Wintergirls* and Laurie Halse Anderson," *Post-Standard*, 27 March 2009, http://blog.syracuse.com/shelflife.

57. Laurie Halse Anderson, "Live Journal," 1 March 2005, http://halseanderson.livejournal.com.

58. Anderson, "Live Journal," 1 March 2005.

59. Laurie Halse Anderson, "Live Journal," 15 February 2008, http://halseanderson.livejournal.com.

60. Laurie Halse Anderson, "Live Journal," 7 May 2005, http://halseanderson.livejournal.com.

61. Laurie Halse Anderson, "Live Journal," 18 January 2009, http://halseanderson.livejournal.com.

62. Anderson, "Live Journal," 18 January 2009.

63. Prince, "Writing from the Heart," 71.

64. Laurie Halse Anderson, "Live Journal," 20 May 2005, http://halseanderson.livejournal.com.

65. Anderson, "Live Journal," 20 May 2005.

66. Anderson, "Live Journal," 20 May 2005.

67. Anderson, "Live Journal," 20 May 2005.

68. Laurie Halse Anderson, "Live Journal," 19 February 2009, http://halseanderson.livejournal.com.

69. Stephanie Holcomb Anderson, "Officially Long Official Biography of Laurie Halse Anderson," *Author Website*, 2008, www.writerlady.com/bioh.html.

70. Larson, "Laurie Halse Anderson Speaks."

Chapter Three

=========================○=========================

Speak

SPEAK IS LAURIE HALSE ANDERSON's best-known and best-selling novel. Since its publication in 1999, more than 1 million paperback copies and 80,000 hardbound copies have been sold. It has garnered an international readership through translations of the text into Catalan, Chinese (Mandarin), Croatian, Danish, Dutch, German, Indonesian, Japanese, Korean, Norwegian, Polish, Serbian, Slovak, Spanish, Swedish, and Thai.

Speak, a *New York Times* best-seller, has been honored multiple times by multiple sources at the national, state, and professional levels. The novel was named an American Library Association Best Book for Young Adults, American Library Association Quick Pick for Young Adults, International Reading Association Young Adult Choice, Junior Library Guild Selection, New York Public Library Book for the Teen Age, and Young Adult Library Services Association Popular Paperback for Young Adults. Among booksellers, the title was recognized as a *Booklist* Editors' Choice, *School Library Journal* Best Book of the Year, *Bulletin of the Center for Children's Books* Blue Ribbon Book, *Horn Book*'s Honor Book, *Los Angeles Times* Award finalist, and a *Publishers Weekly* Bestseller. Perhaps most significantly, *Speak* was awarded the Society of Children's Book Writers and Illustrators Golden Kite Award and named an Edgar Allan Poe Award finalist, a National Book Award finalist, and a Michael L. Printz Honor Book. In their article "The Best Young Adult Novels of All Time," which appeared in the January 2005 issue of *English Journal*, Ted Hipple and Jennifer Claiborne ranked *Speak* as number three. It was also one of the novels considered in the decision to award Anderson the Margaret A.

Edwards award in 2009. (See the appendix for awards and award nominations for this and other titles.) Anderson, however, was shocked when she first learned it was going to be published, much less honored with multiple awards, translated, and integrated into courses taught by teachers around the United States. She says, "I bumbled my way through *Speak*. I didn't really know what I was doing."[1] The first publisher turned down the manuscript, but the editor wrote a personalized rejection letter noting that she appreciated the story although she "didn't like the somewhat quirky narrative style."[2] Anderson persisted; she sent the manuscript to another house where it was then plucked from the slush pile.

THE STORY

Speak tells the story of fourteen-year-old Melinda Sordino, an insightful, wry, and wounded high school student who has a secret she cannot voice: she was raped by an upperclassman at an end-of-summer party. Her decision to call the police abruptly ends the festivities and results in her being ostracized within her school community and among her used-to-be friends. Melinda has no clan in an adolescent world defined by clans; she is socially homeless. Her parents, given their own preoccupation with adult matters of consequence, fail to see Melinda's internal decline, noting only their disappointment in her falling grades and placing blame for Melinda's increasing silence on her or one another. To cope, Melinda closes herself off from others, gnaws at her lips to mask the pain she feels elsewhere, and hides in an abandoned janitor's closet, a place with "no purpose, no name" that reeks of "sour sponges" and decay.[3]

Hope comes in the form of Mr. Freeman, the art teacher who demands that students witness the world through different eyes, recognize the formerly unrecognizable, see what lies beneath. As Melinda struggles and grows as an artist, she gains and gathers the strength necessary to shed her feelings of victimization and blame and fight back in the reclamation of her voice. As the story unfolds in four sections paralleling the four marking periods of the school year, readers bear witness to Melinda's rapid and debilitating descent and eventual rise to an aware and assured self.

REVIEWER RESPONSE

Reviewers found much to praise in this story, calling the novel "a stunning and sympathetic tribute to the teenage outcast,"[4] "a story told with acute insight, acid wit, and affecting prose,"[5] and "an uncannily funny book even as it plumbs the darkness."[6]

Several reviewers commented on Anderson's knack for creating a compelling narrator whose voice is memorable, real, and likely to find resonance among teen readers. They describe Melinda's voice as "bitter, sardonic, and always believable."[7] As one reviewer notes, her pain is "palpable, and readers will totally empathize with her."[8] According to a *Publishers Weekly* reviewer, Anderson "uses keen observations and vivid imagery to pull readers into the head of an isolated teenager. Anderson infuses the narrative with a wit that sustains the heroine through her pain and holds readers' empathy."[9] Still other reviewers argued that this voice has the power to not only engage but affect those who connect with the narrator: "Melinda's voice is distinct, unusual, and very real as she recounts her past and present experiences in bitterly ironic, occasionally even amusing vignettes. Melinda's sarcastic wit, honesty, and courage make her a memorable character whose ultimate triumph will inspire and empower readers."[10] After reading *Speak*, another reviewer concluded, "It will be hard for any teen to look at the class scapegoat again without a measure of compassion and understanding for that person—who may be screaming beneath the silence."[11]

Reviewers also commended Anderson on her ability to create a high school setting that reeks of reality, praising the "bleak, scathingly honest depiction of the world of high school"[12] that "perfectly captures the harsh conformity of high school cliques"[13] and "illustrates the cruelty of peer pressure."[14] According to one reviewer, Anderson "nails the high-school experience cold."[15] In her CNN.com review, Nancy Mattson characterizes Anderson's first novel as a "dead-on portrayal of ostracized 9th-grader Melinda's day-to-day life in the Darwinian world that teen-agers inhabit. . . . [The] novel shows that she understands (and remembers) the raw emotion and tumult that marks the lives of teen-agers."[16] A *Kirkus* reviewer echoes this sentiment, calling the novel "a frightening and sobering look at the cruelty and viciousness that pervade much of contemporary high school life, as real as today's headlines. The plot is gripping and the characters are powerfully drawn, but it is its raw and unvarnished look at the dynamics of the high school experience that makes this a novel that will be hard for readers to forget."[17]

In consideration of the author's craft, reviewers admired Anderson's ability to create a tone and style both unique and appropriate to the narrator's voice and situation. One commented positively on the "sharp, crisp writing that draws readers in, engulfing them in the story."[18] Another argued that "wonderfully descriptive language, along with the suspense, capture and propel the reader through this tale."[19] Yet another admired how the "short, titled passages" give the novel "a stylish contemporary feel" appropriate for the contemporary audience.[20] This sentiment was confirmed by a reviewer for the *Bulletin of the Center for Children's Books* who praised Anderson for letting Melinda tell her story in the way it needed to be told to her adolescent readers; Anderson "doesn't overburden Melinda with insight or with artistic metaphors."[21]

Although *Speak* met with minor faultfinding, every reviewer couched the criticism in positive commentary. One reviewer, for example, called the physical confrontation at the novel's conclusion "dramatically charged and not entirely in keeping with the tone of the rest of the novel" but "satisfying nevertheless."[22] Another confirmed this assessment of the novel's climactic scene that involves Melinda facing her attacker once more by saying this is the "only part of the plot that feels forced."[23] This reviewer also claimed that the novel's symbolism is "sometimes heavy-handed" but "effective." The review ends with an affirmative evaluation: "The book's overall gritty realism and Melinda's hard-won metamorphosis will leave readers touched and inspired."

STORY ORIGINS

Given the extensive praise bestowed on the novel, one might expect *Speak* to have been divinely inspired. Its creation certainly was not calculated or premeditated. It came under the cover of darkness, in a dream, a nightmare. Anderson describes *Speak* as a novel "born out of terror."[24] One night, she awoke and thought she heard the crying of one of her daughters. She went into each of their rooms to check on them but found them sleeping soundly, quiet. Yet the cries of a girl, increasingly hysterical in nature, persevered. The girl sobbed as Anderson put on her robe and went to the computer. It was only when the cursor blinked that her tears subsided.

Anderson remembers the moment she met her protagonist, Melinda Sordino: "She made a tapping noise and blew into a microphone. 'Is this thing
on?' she asked. 'I have a story to tell you.'"[25]
    Several forces might explain the arrival of this girl, this story, on the
author's mental doorstep. Anderson's oldest daughter was in sixth grade at
the time and undergoing the physical and emotional changes brought on
by adolescence. Witnessing this transformation unfold in her daughter's
life called forth teenage memories Anderson had attempted to suppress
for years. Simultaneously, Anderson was reading adolescent psychothera-
pist Mary Pipher's *Reviving Ophelia*, whose text draws from anecdotal
evidence, research findings, and case examples to argue that today's teenage girls are coming of age in a society that continues to diminish them
as females. Anderson says, "The issues of growth, and girls who won't, or
can't, speak up for themselves were cooking in the back of my mind."[26]
She was supposed to be writing about the Irish potato famine that oc-
curred in the 1840s, but Melinda's story "had nothing to do with Ireland
or famine ships. This was a 'today' story, bitter and cold."[27]
    In addition to finding inspiration in her protagonist's compelling voice,
Anderson was also motivated to write Melinda's story because, at least on
an emotional level, it parallels her own high school experience and embodies much of what she identifies as problematic about this experience for
teens in general. The world of high school, she explains, "seems uniquely
tailored to damage children."[28] Anderson insists that *Speak* is indeed a fictional work but recognizes that elements of Melinda's emotional journey
reflect her own sense of self as a fourteen-year-old,[29] particularly "the way
she is confused and filled with doubts (and occasionally self-loathing)."[30]
"Feeling isolated," she adds, "gave me (and Melinda) a useful perspective
on the absurdities of high school culture."[31]

WRITING THE NOVEL

Anderson describes *Speak* as "the least deliberately written book" she's
ever created.[32] The first draft took a few months to complete, and the
requisite seven drafts followed, resulting in a process that took one year
from start to finish. She did very little research in the writing of the novel,
drawing instead on knowledge garnered through visits to large suburban
schools during her tenure as a newspaper reporter, as well as regular jaunts

to Taco Bell and the mall to learn more about what her potential readers talked about and how they talked about it.[33]

This lack of deliberation resulted in a few surprises for the author, including the final incarnation of Melinda's character. Anderson knew much about her protagonist, given her insistent and persistent voice. She explains, "Melinda's voice rang clear as a bell for me. She was angry, bitter, hurt, and funny as hell. She was like a burn victim forced to wear a wool sweater, raw everywhere, and made hyper-observant by her pain."[34] Yet, it wasn't until Anderson was well into the novel that she realized Melinda was an artist, "an artist without a voice, unable to express herself or communicate her pain."[35]

Anderson was also unsure about how the relationship between Melinda and her art teacher, Mr. Freeman, would develop. Although uncertain about how these two characters might influence one another, she determined that it was her job "to type, not analyze."[36] With time and more typing, she realized that Mr. Freeman would serve as the person who "helps Melinda free herself from her prison of silence." In contrast to the other teachers in the story who bear disparaging nicknames, Melinda calls Mr. Freeman by his full name, thus indicating the high esteem in which she holds him.[37]

Anderson faced additional surprises in the determination of the novel's format and guiding symbols. After completing the portion set during the first marking period, she toyed with Melinda's character by jotting down some notes as she imagined how her report card might look. As she engaged in this process, the eventual structure of the novel became clear: "four marking periods, four report cards, a school year from the first day to the last."[38] Similarly, Anderson didn't set out to use the image of a tree as a symbolic representation of Melinda's growth and maturation over time. "A tree showed up in the first draft and I ran with it," she explains.[39] The idea for the tree as the focus of Melinda's art project resulted from her own frustrated attempts to carve a tree out of a linoleum block over the course of several months during her ninth grade art class. This, she says, was the conscious decision. Her subconscious, what Anderson calls "the smart part," took over from there. It wasn't until she was revising that she identified the potential symbolic import of the image. She uttered a "duh" and "tweaked the manuscript so that the current ran through the story cleanly."[40]

Creating a satisfactory ending required, too, that Anderson open herself to the unexpected. It took three endings—and repeated encouragement from her editor—before she got it right. Anderson attributes the need for multiple incarnations of the novel's final moment to her unwillingness to allow Melinda to face potential pain. "I was too protective of Mellie," she explains. "I didn't want her to get hurt again; I couldn't stand the thought of leaving her unprotected."[41] Anderson realized, however, that she had no other choice if she wanted to be true to the character whose voice had woken something in her as a listener, a writer. Melinda had to find her voice. Once Anderson came to this understanding, the novel's necessary conclusion became clear. Anderson describes this moment: "I saw the whole thing, smelled it, felt my heart thumping. I was scared. So was Mellie. And then, that voice. She claimed it, claimed herself as worthy and strong enough to fight back. She screamed the house down and saved herself, scarred, bloody, and alive."[42]

Anderson chuckles when she receives reader questions regarding the level of intention employed in the novel. One teacher, for example, noted that the novel begins and ends with the word "it," the same name Melinda gives her attacker. Anderson wishes she could say, "Oh, yeah, I totally planned that. I'm so smart,"[43] but she can't—and won't.

As Anderson nears the completion of the revision process in any given piece, she considers explicitly the intended audience, ensuring that the language, images, and other elements are appropriate and accessible to the readers she expects will pick up the book. Given its emotionally charged content, Anderson was particularly deliberate in her revision decisions in *Speak*. She wanted the novel to be well suited for a wide range of teens, including those at the younger end of the spectrum, given the fact that "so many young teens are sexually assaulted; they are easy targets because they are young and naïve."[44] As a result, Anderson toned down Melinda's memory of the rape, making it less graphic. She feels this revision "works organically within the story" because when Melinda was raped, she was under the influence of alcohol, thus creating a memory that is a "little blurred around the edges."[45]

READER RESPONSE

Given Anderson's keen awareness and attention to her intended audience, she is wholly interested in their reaction to what she's written—and couldn't be more satisfied with how they have responded to *Speak*. She commends readers for their willingness to learn, to develop "a new understanding of sexual assault and depression" as a result of engaging with the text. She celebrates survivors of sexual assault who, in response to Melinda's story, "dug deep and found the courage to speak up about their own pain." And she credits the teachers and administrators who made this possible by putting the book "where it could open minds and hearts."[46]

While Anderson appreciates the fact that her novel has garnered such overwhelming positive professional reviews, she is even more validated by the programs that have resulted from it. She cites the 2005 "One Book, One Community"[47] project organized in Appleton, Wisconsin, by the town's public librarians, in which members of the community were invited to read and discuss the novel. As Anderson describes it:

> They got the Mayor on board, the police department, the schools, the education foundation. Book clubs read the book. Senior citizens in nursing homes read the book. Countless teens and parents read it. People talked about it in church groups. In car pools. Over coffee. Tee-shirts and lawn signs (lawn signs!) were made promoting the project. Everyone wore buttons. There was a billboard. Strangers talked to each other about it in grocery stores and in lines at the bank.

For Anderson, the real significance of this project is that "in America, in 2005, a Mid-Western community came together—all ages, all facets of society—to talk about a contemporary YA story."

Anderson attributes the novel's appeal for so many readers to its treatment of depression, not rape. She argues that almost every young person in America "has gotten to that ugly, gloomy, dark hole that they can't find a way out of" and describes letters from readers who relate to Melinda's sense of helplessness regardless of how these feelings were engendered. Anderson's mailbox is filled with letters that read something like, "Ok, like, I'm the biggest jock of the school and if you ever tell anybody this I'll kill you, but I know exactly what that girl feels like."[48]

Teen readers have found such connection to Melinda's voice and resonance in her story that they don't want it to end. Many have requested a sequel. Anderson, however, is reluctant to honor this request. She says she would love to write another novel that allows her to hang out with Melinda but claims "it's up to her. If I try to resurrect her just to hammer out a sequel, it will be awful. You have to respect your characters as much as you do your friends."[49] So far, Melinda has found her way into just one of Anderson's other novels; she makes a cameo appearance in *Catalyst*.

SPEAK UP ABOUT SPEAK

In 2009, to celebrate the influence of *Speak* on young adult readers and the larger field of young adult literature, Penguin Puffin issued a tenth anniversary edition containing a new interview with Anderson. In addition, readers were invited to visit a Speak Up About Speak Blog[50] to share their responses to the text and personal experiences in dealing with issues highlighted in the novel. Anderson also wrote a poem, the first she's ever made available to the reading public. Entitled "Listen," the piece begins and ends with Anderson's words, while the stanzas in between contain words drawn from letters or e-mail messages she has received from readers since the original publication of *Speak*. (The poem is printed in its entirety in chapter 11 of this text.)

These efforts align with Anderson's continued assertion that you can't block pain. "It's like a river—block it one place and it floods somewhere else. Try and hide from your pain and it'll hurt you in a different place."[51] She tells teens that they have a choice in how they will deal with their pain: control it by dealing with it, or ignore it and be controlled by it. Speak up, she invokes. Be heard, she urges. Stop hurting yourselves, she begs. Someone will listen, she assures.[52]

ACADEMIC RESPONSE

Speak has generated more academic response than any other novel Anderson has written. In addition to literary analysis, scholars have considered how it might be set to pedagogical use in the classroom.

Literary Analysis

Several scholars have analyzed *Speak* through a feminist lens, arguing that the novel explores and critiques gender expectations in a patriarchal world. Sally Smith argues that Melinda is "aware of cultural expectations for femininity, the rigid prescriptions for female attractiveness, for female friendship and gossip, for being a 'good' girl."[53] She is unable to negotiate these expectations, however, when she loses confidence in herself as a result of the rape and finds no support in the school or social environments that prove complicit in the creation of Melinda's alienation.

Marsha Sprague and Kara Keeling apply feminist thinking in their brief comparison of the protagonists in Beverly Cleary's *Fifteen* and Anderson's *Speak* in an examination of how the two novels, "both centered on the experiences of high school girls, reveal dramatic changes in the social fabric of the United States from the mid-1950s to the end of the 20th century, particularly in the ways that adolescent girls come of age."[54] Similarly, Elizabeth Boyd compares the female protagonists in *Speak* and Nikki Grimes's *Bronx Masquerade*, arguing that, in both novels, the protagonists find their voices "through their creative expressions, developing confidence in a protected space and then asserting themselves outside of this space."[55] Carla Verderame examines the ways in which the female narrators in *Speak* and Carson McCullers's *The Member of the Wedding* "learn to write their own stories, to assert their own voice . . . [and] to establish their own positions in a patriarchal world" despite the fact that they live in different parts of the country, come of age at different times, and conform to expectations differently.[56]

Melissa Ames extends this feminist analysis by analyzing how Anderson uses the public bathroom in the high school as a gendered space. She explains how women have been socialized to view the public restroom as a site for crying, a confessional, or a sanctuary. She argues that Anderson's use of the space demonstrates how the "women's restroom is actually an ideal site for the developing of a feminist politics and the housing of oppositional art."[57] Ames cites the graffiti posted on the bathroom wall regarding Andy Evans as evidence of the bathroom stall as a space where women can talk to one another and talk back.

Other scholars have considered *Speak* through the lens of gay, lesbian, bisexual, and transgendered theories. Don Latham argues that the novel can be read as a coming-out story. After the rape, he explains, Melinda "retreats—literally and metaphorically—into a closet in order to keep people from learning the truth and to help her cope with her trauma."[58] Over the duration of the novel, Melinda suppresses her voice as a means to recover (and discover) a voice that can speak the truth. Melinda's story, says Latham, represents the view from the closet, one that "questions and subverts dominant heterosexist assumptions about gender, identity, and trauma." Melinda learns that gender and identity are "neither essential nor fixed" but are instead "a proliferation of performances," thus allowing her to face that which awaits her on the other side of the door, a strategy that might offer liberating potential for adolescent readers.

Still other scholars have included *Speak* in the cross-examination of several young adult titles that share certain themes or elements. Jean Dimmitt analyzes each of the 2000 Printz award finalists, concluding that each involves the development of three big ideas: the search for self, friendship, and truth. In *Speak*, Melinda must acquire self-knowledge in order to talk about what happened on the lawn that night, demonstrate a capacity for friendship in the warning she offers Rachel despite the fragility of their relationship, and recognize the truth regarding the rape—she was not to blame.[59] Jennifer Miskec and Chris McGee engage in similar processes but instead examine cutting as a form of self-mutilation in several young adult novels. With respect to *Speak*, the authors describe the scene in which Melinda slides the paperclip over the inside of her wrist and says, "Pitiful. If a suicide attempt is a cry for help, then what is this? A whimper, a peep?" Miskec and McGee see this "quick and sole experience with cutting" as evidence of Melinda's "keen awareness" and "dismissal of the outdated medication language that connects cutting with suicide."[60]

Pedagogical Promise

In addition to analyzing *Speak* as a literary text, several scholars have considered how it might be used in the classroom setting for different purposes. C. J. Bott advocates for the use of *Speak* as a classroom text that demonstrates survival and strength in response to sexual assault. "How many of our female students need to arm-wrestle some demons and think it is too impossible to try?" she asks. "Imagine how Melinda's courage might inspire them."[61]

Other researchers argue that the text might be used among classroom students to foster a critical stance. Mary Ann Tighe sees potential in the novel's ability to encourage readers to consider societal expectations, the influence of conformity, the necessity of parental support, and the means to survival in their lives beyond the text. Similarly, Janet Alsup encourages teachers to use *Speak* to confront difficult topics and encourage a critical stance in teen readers. Literature such as this, she argues, allows teens to "release tensions," to talk about issues that are uncomfortable or embarrassing.[62]

English teacher Mark Jackett used *Speak* to foster discussion of complex and sometimes uncomfortable issues in his ninth grade class. At the university level, sj Miller used *Speak* in a young adult methods course to demonstrate how teachers might create transformative and liberating experiences for students focused on modeling teaching strategies, applying them in small co-teaching groups, and reflecting on the experience. Similarly, Martha Sprague, Kara Keeling, and Paul Lawrence asked teachers enrolled in a graduate program and high school students to compare their impressions of Beverly Cleary's *Fifteen* and Anderson's *Speak*. While teachers "sought illumination from the texts that would help them understand the world of the students that they were teaching," students "were more focused on the micro-themes related to their own world."[63]

Two published works focus on the artistic elements of *Speak* and the potential for such to encourage critical thought or personal healing. Judith Franzak and Elizabeth Noll suggest that teachers use the novel to engage students in critical inquiry of the violence it portrays. They might allow students to use several artistic media to create works that represent an "aspect of silencing in their own lives," for example, or research "the link between artists and depression."[64] Diane Ressler and Stan Giannet argue for the use of *Speak* as a creative artifact, one that might inspire expression in readers in therapeutic ways. Creative expression therapies, they insist, might help people, particularly adolescents dealing with difficult situations, "find their own speaking voices and use them to begin healing."[65]

OTHER ITERATIONS OF THE NOVEL

On 9–10 November 2007, *Speak* underwent a transformation in its rebirth from novel to stage play. Directed by Steve Braddock, the production premiered at Anderson's alma mater, Fayetteville-Manlius High School, and was soon thereafter brought to the stage at the neighboring Nottingham High School. Anderson was flattered by the project—and terrified to attend the production. Revisiting the site of her own high school struggles proved to be emotionally daunting. "It still smells the same," she reported. As she entered the lobby, she almost retreated, but with her husband by her side, she found the way to her seat. "I dug my fingernails into my palm and sat down in the auditorium where I had spent so many miserable hours. I focused on not hyperventilating," she says. But the experience was ultimately liberating, helping her replace painful memories in this place with more constructive and positive ones. "The kids saved me," Anderson says, "Totally saved me, grabbed my heart, cradled it and made me proud to be connected to them."[66]

Speak was also adapted for film. The screenplay was co-written by Jessica Sharzer (who also directed) and Annie Young Frisbie, and it stars Kristen Stewart (of Twilight fame) as Melinda, Michael Angarano as David Petrakis, Robert John Burke as Mr. Neck, Hallee Hirsh as Rachel, Eric Lively as Andy Evans, Leslie Lyles as Hairwoman, Elizabeth Perkins as Melinda's mother, Allison Silko as Heather, D. B. Sweeney as Melinda's father, and Steve Zahn as Mr. Freeman.

The film premiered at the Sundance Film Festival in 2004, won the Audience Award at the Woodstock Film Festival in 2004, and was nominated for the Writers Guild of America Award in 2006. The Directors Guild of America also nominated Jessica Sharzer for an Outstanding Directorial Achievement in Children's Programs Award in 2006. On 5 September 2005, the film aired on television; it was broadcast simultaneously on the Showtime and Lifetime cable channels. Entertainment Weekly selected the film as a "Must Watch" the week it aired, awarding it a grade of "B+."[67]

Writer/director Sharzer had a budget of $1 million, one camera, and three weeks to make the movie. These limitations—and Sharzer's creative response to them—made the movie all the more effective. She cast her film with intention, selecting younger, less well-known actors who credibly looked the right age. As Sharzer explains, "I really wanted to believe that they were either just on the cusp of puberty, or just experiencing it, because that's very much where this movie lives and breathes, in that transitional moment of life."[68] She also chose to shoot the film in a real high school with real kids in Columbus, Ohio, not the typical choice for a Hollywood film. "You can smell the cafeteria in our movie," Sharzer says with pride.[69]

Anderson responded very favorably to the film adaptation of her novel. She was asked to collaborate on the screenplay but, due to other writing obligations, felt compelled to decline the offer. Although she wasn't involved in the writing, she describes the movie as "very faithful to the book," even though some things had to be cut or adapted in the transition between genres. "Because the film cannot capture the running interior monologue of my intensely first person novel," Anderson says, "film watchers miss out on the funnier elements of Melinda, and I think her growth comes across a bit choppy on screen. But I don't have a problem with it."[70]

Anderson and her daughter Stephanie visited the set for two days and watched in awe as the director and performers dealt with unforeseen challenges. Although summer temperatures were scorching, for example, the air conditioning on the set had to be turned off, as the noise it generated negatively affected the sound recording. Another day saw the loss of power due to a thunderstorm that also resulted in holes in the school's roof. Anderson's experiences with the cast and crew were nothing but positive, although Anderson admits that whenever Mr. Neck walked in the room, her "stomach started to hurt. Even though he was sweet off camera, his on-camera role was intense."[71] Anderson found much to admire in Kristen Stewart's portrayal of Melinda and believes she had the most difficult role in that she was required to show her character's emotions without being able to use many words. Anderson learned to admire the performers even more when she was cast to play a small role in the film as the lunch lady in the cafeteria: "All I had to do was drop mashed potatoes on a plate, and it took seven takes. It made me realize I shouldn't give up my day job."[72]

The airing of the film on both networks was followed by a public service announcement from the Rape, Abuse, and Incest National Network, informing viewers of the resources available to victims of sexual assault and other forms of abuse. The National Sexual Assault Hotline reported an increase of over 600 percent in calls following the first East Coast showing of the film. That made the experience all the more meaningful for Anderson.[73]

NOTES

1. Laurie Halse Anderson, "Speaking Truth to Power," speech delivered at the Annual Workshop of the Assembly on Literature for Adolescents, San Antonio, Texas, 15 November 2008.

2. Little Willow, "Interview: Laurie Halse Anderson," *Slayground*, 5 August 2007, http://slayground.livejournal.com.

3. Laurie Halse Anderson, *Speak* (New York: Farrar, Straus and Giroux, 1999), 25–26.

4. Jennifer Hubert, *Amazon.com* Review, www.amazon.com.

5. *Library Journal* 21 (October 1999).
6. Lauren Adams, *Horn Book Magazine* 75, no. 5 (1999): 605–6.
7. Paula Rohrlick, *Kliatt* (September 1999): 4.
8. Dina Sherman, *School Library Journal* (October 1999): 144.
9. *Publishers Weekly*, 13 September 1999, 85.
10. Debbie Carton, *Booklist*, 15 September 1999, 247.
11. Hubert.
12. Rohrlick, 4.
13. Stephanie Zvirin, *Booklist*, 15 November 2000, 632.
14. Jennifer Ralston, *School Library Journal* (October 2003): 99.
15. Adams, 605–6.
16. Nancy Mattson, *CNN.com*, 29 November 1999, www.cnn.com.
17. *Kirkus Reviews*, 19 September 1999, 1496.
18. Sherman, 144.
19. Katherine Barr, *ALAN Review* 27, no. 2 (2000).
20. Maggie Meacham, *Children's Literature*, 2000, http://childrenslit.com.
21. *Bulletin of the Center for Children's Books* (October 1999): 45.
22. Adams, 605–6.
23. *Publishers Weekly*, 85.
24. Laurie Halse Anderson, "Speaking Out," *ALAN Review* 27, no. 3 (2000): 25–26.
25. Anderson, "Speaking Out," 25–26.
26. Anderson, "Speaking Out," 25–26.
27. Anderson, "Speaking Out," 25–26.
28. "Laurie Halse Anderson Chats with Readergirlz," *Readergirlz*, 23 June 2008, www.mitaliblog.com/search/label/Author%20Interviews.
29. Laurie Halse Anderson, "Frequently Asked Questions," *Author Website*, www.writerlady.com/faqh.html.
30. Laurie Halse Anderson, "Live Journal," 25 March 2005, http://halseanderson.livejournal.com.
31. Laurie Halse Anderson, "Interview with the Author," in *Speak* (New York: Penguin, 2009), Bonus Material.
32. Jennifer M. Brown, "In Dreams Begin Possibilities," in "Flying Starts: Six Authors and Illustrators with Well-Received Fall Debuts Talk about Their Work," *Publisher's Weekly*, 20 December 1999, 24–25.
33. Laurie Halse Anderson, "Live Journal," 20 May 2005, http://halseanderson.livejournal.com.
34. Anderson, "Speaking Out," 25–26.
35. Anderson, "Speaking Out," 25–26.
36. Anderson, "Speaking Out," 25–26.
37. Laurie Halse Anderson, "Live Journal," 3 February 2005, http://halseanderson.livejournal.com.

38. Anderson, "Speaking Out," 25–26.

39. Laurie Halse Anderson, "Live Journal," 20 May 2005, http://halseanderson.livejournal.com.

40. Dana Schwartz, "Interview with Laurie Halse Anderson," *Book Bag*, available at www.teenreads.com/authors.

41. Anderson, "Speaking Out," 25–26.

42. Anderson, "Speaking Out," 25–26.

43. Laurie Halse Anderson, "Live Journal," 2 June 2005, http://halseanderson.livejournal.com.

44. Laurie Halse Anderson, "Live Journal," 4 March 2009, http://halseanderson.livejournal.com.

45. Anderson, "Live Journal," 4 March 2009.

46. Little Willow, "Interview: Laurie Halse Anderson."

47. Laurie Halse Anderson, "Live Journal," 19 April 2005, http://halseanderson.livejournal.com.

48. Laurie Halse Anderson, "Loving the Young Adult Reader Even When You Want to Strangle Him (or Her)!" *ALAN Review* 32, no. 2 (2005): 53–58.

49. Schwartz, "Interview with Laurie Halse Anderson."

50. See http://speakupaboutspeak.blogspot.com.

51. Schwartz, "Interview with Laurie Halse Anderson."

52. Laurie Halse Anderson, "Live Journal," 25 March 2005, http://halseanderson.livejournal.com.

53. Sally Smith, *Journal of Adolescent and Adult Literacy* 43, no. 6 (2000): 585.

54. Marsha K. Sprague and Kara K. Keeling, "From *Fifteen* to *Speak*: Challenges Facing the Adolescent Girl in U.S. Society," in *Discovering Their Voices: Engaging Adolescent Girls with Young Adult Literature* (Newark, Del.: International Reading Association, 2007), 4.

55. Elizabeth Meckley Boyd, "Lost and Found: Female Voice in Laurie Halse Anderson's *Speak* and Nikki Grimes' *Bronx Masquerade*," master's thesis, University of North Carolina, Charlotte, 2006.

56. Carla L. Verderame, "Out of Silence into Speech: Two Perspectives of Growing Up Female," *ALAN Review* 28, no. 1 (2000): 2.

57. Melissa Ames, "Memoirs of a Bathroom Stall: The Women's Lavatory as Crying Room, Confessional, and Sanctuary," *EAPSU Online: A Journal of Critical and Creative Work* 3 (Fall 2006): 63–64.

58. Don Latham, "Melinda's Closet: Trauma and the Queer Subtext of Laurie Halse Anderson's *Speak*," *Children's Literature Association Quarterly* 31, no. 4 (2006): 369.

59. Jean Pollard Dimmitt, "The First Printz Award Designations: Winners All," *ALAN Review* 28, no. 2 (2001): 54–59.

60. Jennifer Miskec and Chris McGee, "My Scars Tell a Story: Self-Mutilation in Young Adult Literature," *Children's Literature Association Quarterly* 32, no. 2 (2007): 167.

61. C. J. Bott, "Why We Must Read Young Adult Books That Deal with Sexual Content," *ALAN Review* 34, no. 3 (2006): 26–29.

62. Mary Ann Tighe, "Reviving Ophelia with Young Adult Literature," *ALAN Review* 33, no. 1 (2005): 56–61; Janet Alsup, "Politicizing Young Adult Literature: Reading Anderson's *Speak* as a Critical Text," *Journal of Adolescent and Adult Literacy* 47, no.2 (2003): 160.

63. Mark Jackett, "Something to *Speak* About: Addressing Sensitive Issues through Literature," *English Journal* 96, no. 4 (2007): 102–5; sj Miller, "'Speaking' the Walk, 'Speaking' the Talk: Embodying Critical Pedagogy to Teach Young Adult Literature," *English Education* 40, no. 2 (2008): 145–54; Marsha M. Sprague, Kara K. Keeling, and Paul Lawrence, "'Today I'm going to meet a boy': Teachers and Students Respond to *Fifteen* and *Speak*," *ALAN Review* 34, no. 1 (2006): 25–31.

64. Judith Franzak and Elizabeth Noll, "Monstrous Acts: Problematizing Violence in Young Adult Literature," *Journal of Adolescent and Adult Literacy* 49, no. 8 (2006): 668.

65. Diane Ressler and Stan Giannet, "Voices of Healing: How Creative Expression Therapies Help Us Heal, Using Laurie Halse Anderson's Novel, *Speak*, as a Springboard for Discussion," in *Using Literature to Help Troubled Teenagers Cope with Abuse Issues*, ed. Joan F. Kaywell (Westport, Conn.: Greenwood, 2004), 186.

66. Laurie Halse Anderson, "Live Journal," 10 November 2007, http://halseanderson.livejournal.com.

67. Laurie Halse Anderson, "Live Journal," 4 September 2005, http://halseanderson.livejournal.com.

68. John Crook, "*Speak* Loud Enough for Showtime/Lifetime," *National Society of Film Critics*, 3 September 2005, http://tv.zap2it.com/tveditorial.

69. Crook, "*Speak* Loud Enough for Showtime/Lifetime."

70. Carol Fitzgerald and Marisa Emralino, "Interview with Laurie Halse Anderson," *Teenreads.com*, August 2005, www.teenreads.com/authors.

71. Laurie Halse Anderson, "Live Journal," 18 September 2005, http://halseanderson.livejournal.com.

72. Linda M. Castellitto, "Making History Come Alive for Young Readers," *First Person Book Page*, November 2008, www.bookpage.com.

73. Anderson, "Live Journal," 18 September 2005.

Chapter Four

===========================O===========================

Fever 1793

ANDERSON BEGAN WORK on *Fever 1793* in 1993. The novel wasn't completed and published until 2000, however, due to Anderson's nighttime visit from Melinda Sordino and the resulting urge to put that story on paper and set the historical novel aside. The wait proved worthwhile; her recreation of life in Philadelphia during a yellow fever epidemic was well received.

Fever 1793 earned several national accolades. It was named an American Library Association Best Book for Young Adults, International Reading Association Teacher's Choice, Parent's Guide to Children's Media Award winner, Jefferson Cup Honor Book for Historical Fiction, Junior Library Guild Selection, and Children's Book-of-the-Month Club selection, and it was listed as one of the New York Public Library's 100 Best Books and the New York Public Library Best Books for the Teen Age. At the state level, the novel earned the Rebecca Caudill Award (Illinois) and Great Lakes' Great Books Award (Michigan) and was named a Massachusetts Children's Book Award Honor Book, Volunteer State Book Award runner-up (Tennessee), and Tayshas High School Reading List (Texas) title. Among booksellers, the novel was cited as an American Bookseller Pick of the Lists and *Publishers Weekly* Bestseller. (See the appendix for other award nominations for this title.)

Professional reviews mirrored this positive response. Critics called the novel "a thrilling story about a gutsy teenager,"[1] a "harrowing historical novel,"[2] and "a riveting and well-researched historical fiction."[3] Another described the novel as "a vivid work, rich with well-drawn and believable characters. Unexpected events pepper the top-flight novel that combines accurate historical detail with a spellbinding story line."[4] "Anderson," yet another reviewer said, "has fashioned a gripping story about living morally under the shadow of rampant death."[5] Readers "will be drawn in by the characters and will emerge with a sharp and graphic picture of another world"[6] and "find this a gripping picture of disease's devastating effect on people, and on the social fabric itself."[7]

Reviewers were particularly taken with Anderson's portrayal of Mattie, the novel's "tenacious and tenderhearted" protagonist.[8] They admired Anderson's ability to create a believable character in a time and place far removed from the reality of her contemporary audience: "Ambitious, resentful of the ordinary tedium of her life, and romantically imaginative, Matilda is a believable teenager, so immersed in her own problems that she can describe the freed and widowed slave who works for her family as the 'luckiest' person she knows."[9] Anderson goes "back in time" to create a strong heroine whose story remains believable despite her many trials.[10] Additionally, critics identified and valued the realistic growth Mattie demonstrates over the course of the novel, noting how her "sufferings have changed her from a willful child to a strong, capable young woman able to manage her family's business on her own."[11] This coming-of-age tale "succeeds in conveying both [Mattie's] strong-willed spirit and the difficulties of life in that era, when daily work was ceaseless and backbreaking. Mattie changes convincingly from a resentful teenager to a responsible adult over the course of a few months, as the dreadful events around her force her to grow up."[12]

Anderson prides herself on the quality of research she conducts in preparation for her historical fiction. She must have smiled when she read reviews that addressed this element of *Fever 1793*. Critics described the work as "carefully researched,"[13] capturing vividly "the sights, sounds, and smells of Philadelphia when it was still the nation's capital."[14] They pointed, too, to the value of the appendix following the story that confirms the historical facts and "adds verisimilitude to Anderson's fictional depiction of period medical procedures."[15] Anderson is also praised for her ability to infuse the story "with rich details of time and place, including some perspective on the little-known role African Americans played in caring for fever victims. . . . Anderson tells a good story and certainly proves you can learn a lot about history in good fiction."[16]

Ironically, the only significant criticism of the novel came in response to its richness of historical detail. A *Publishers Weekly* reviewer argued that, at times, "Mattie's character development, as well as those of her grandfather and widowed mother, takes a back seat to the historical details of Philadelphia and environs."[17] Although commending the novel as "extremely well researched" and commending the way Anderson paints "a vivid picture of the seedy waterfront, the devastation the disease wreaks on a once thriving city, and the bitterness of neighbor toward neighbor as those suspected of infection are physically cast aside," the reviewer found that "these larger scale views" (the return of George Washington to Philadelphia, for example) take precedence over the more intimate scenes designed to provide insight into character. Another reviewer worried that "such a wealth of historical information" led to a less involving plot in which Mattie's "adventures are a series of episodes only casually related to the slender narrative arc in which she wonders if her mother has survived the fever and whether they will be reunited."[18]

THE STORY

Fever 1793 centers on Mattie Cook, a feisty fourteen-year-old who reluctantly helps her mother run a coffeehouse in Philadelphia during the summer of 1793. Her father, who built their home and opened the business when Mattie was four years old, suffered an early death when he fell from a ladder. Mattie's grandfather, Captain William Farnsworth Cook of the Pennsylvania Fifth Regiment, served under General Washington during the Revolutionary War and keeps an eye on Mattie and her mother. Eliza, a free black whose home-style cooking keeps patrons coming back for more, joins the family as an employee. Mattie assumes ample responsibility for the business but eagerly awaits the opportunity to visit the market or pass the home of the famous American painter Charles Willson Peale, who employs young Nathaniel Benson, an artist's assistant Mattie hopes to marry one day.

When reports of fever begin to spread throughout the city and the Cooks lose Polly, their serving girl, to the mysterious disease, panic and fear abound. Those with means leave Philadelphia to seek fresh air and presumed protection in the country. When Mattie's mother falls ill, she insists that her daughter leave town and forces Grandfather Cook to escort her to the home of a family of pig farmers willing to take her in as a helper. On the journey, however, Mattie and her grandfather find themselves stranded. The grandfather falls ill, leaving Mattie alone in the attempt to maintain his health and their survival. Although Mattie, too, succumbs to disease, her grandfather's quick thinking and the support of a wise French doctor keep her alive and able to return to the city.

Upon arriving in her now ravaged city, Mattie finds her mother gone and her shop destroyed. Rather than give up, however, she rises to the challenge in multiple ways. She fights off looters, buries her grandfather after he dies of a heart attack, takes in the orphaned child Nell, gives back to the community by helping Eliza as a member of the Free African Society, and nurses Eliza's nephews and Nell back to health. When the frost finally arrives and the epidemic ends, Mattie and Eliza join forces to reopen the coffeehouse, and she and Nathaniel begin to forge a romantic relationship. Mattie's mother returns home a weakened and dependent woman, a reality Mattie is now ready to face, given the strength she acquired in the face of difficulty.

STORY ORIGINS AND PERSONAL CONNECTIONS

Anderson determined to write a novel about the yellow fever after reading an article about the epidemic in the *Philadelphia Inquirer* in August 1993. She remembers the moment: "I was stunned—I had never heard of the epidemic, and American history is my hobby. When I read about the courage of the people who struggled to survive those days, I knew I had to write about it."[19] Inspired by the strength of everyday people and motivated to share their story, she embarked on a process of recreating this story for teen readers.

This journey required Anderson to immerse herself in the history of this time and place. She visited period houses and museums to learn more about the furniture and clothing used and worn by Philadelphians in the late 1700s and drew knowledge from countless letters, diaries, and newspapers written and published at the time to gain insight into the daily lives of residents—"the sounds of the marketplace and the smells of the sickroom."[20] In her essay "Up for Discussion—The Writing of *Fever 1793*: A Historical Detective Searches for the Truth," Anderson describes the research process as similar to that of an archaeological dig. She began with background reading ("politics of the era, architecture, religion, food, class structure, the social roles of taverns and coffeehouses, education levels, and gardening"). When she sharpened a goose quill and attempted to write with it, her family bandied about the label "obsessive." Anderson, however, dug deeper, finding period maps and annual cities' directories that allowed her to generate a map of her own that she hung above her desk. She then turned her attention to primary source documents—letters, diaries, and account books, the most useful finds in the excavation process that gave Anderson real insight into the lives people lived at this time.[21]

As Anderson began writing, Mattie's story was set apart from her own, distanced from the everyday life she led off the page. When Anderson's mother became ill, however, she found the resulting emotions seeping into the story, particularly during the scenes in which Mattie's mother suffers from the disease.[22] Anderson drew on universally experienced emotions to help bridge the gap between Mattie's story and the one she was working to create for modern readers, spanning the distance between generations through reference to the shared human condition.

INFUSING HISTORY INTO FICTION

In the process of drafting and revising her historical fiction, Anderson commits to telling two stories rather than one—that of the protagonist and that of the time and place in which she lives. In *Fever 1793*, Anderson calls the events of the yellow fever epidemic that raced through Philadelphia the "exterior plot."[23] At the same time, there is the interior plot delineated by Mattie's growth. As the novel opens, Mattie is what Anderson describes as a "likable, but slightly lazy and ornery teenager."[24] As the novel progresses, however, she copes with the realities of the epidemic, thus linking the two stories in the mind of the reader. Anderson likens this dual process to "writing outside of one's culture. The author must be scrupulous about detail and motivation, sensitive to cultural (and time) differences, wary of interpretation, and conscious of the reader's background and ability."[25]

Anderson uses her historical fiction to educate readers through the telling of a compelling story, immersing students in the words and daily rituals of those who lived well before they were born. She begins each chapter with a quotation taken from a primary source document—journal entry, letter, cookbook, or manual. These words put readers in the midst of these happenings. Readers learn, for example, of the glory that was once Philadelphia when they read the opening excerpt from Lord Adam

Gordon's journal, dated 1765: "The city of Philadelphia is perhaps one of the wonders of the world."[26] They are privy to the daily lives of women when they discover a recipe for bread from Amelia Simmons's *American Cookbook*, dated 1796. They consider gender expectations and the resulting rules for girls as described in *The Young Lady Abroad or Affectionate Advice on the Social and Moral Habits of Females*, dated 1777: "A low voice and soft address are the common indications of a well-bred woman."[27] And they witness the results of the fever on the community in a letter from Dr. Benjamin Rush, dated 1793: "There is great distress in the city for want of cash. Friendship is nearly entirely banished from our city."[28]

Anderson supplements this immersion experience with the inclusion of historical context in a comprehensive appendix. She shares biographical information about doctors of the time, namely Rush and Dr. Jean Deverze, and the varying methods they employed in the treatment of patients. She paints a picture of villagers clinging desperately to unscientific methods in the attempt to rid their community of disease—sponges soaked in vinegar and held to the nose, garlic hung around the neck, and mattresses buried underground to destroy any lingering trace of illness. She pays tribute to victims buried in unmarked graves in the old potter's field, now Washington Square. She notes the influence of the Peale family and their contributions not only to the world of painting but natural history as well. She sheds light onto the little-known Free African Society, whose members aided victims, both black and white, in a time of need. She describes the dependence of urban dwellers on the market and the farmers who brought their wares into town each week. And she reminds readers that yellow fever thrives in parts of the world even today, killing thousands each year in sub-Saharan Africa and parts of South America.

SURPRISES AND REVISIONS

In the process of weaving together a compelling story and the history that undergirds it, Anderson faced several choices that sometimes led to unexpected outcomes. She originally envisioned Mattie as a ten-year-old orphan, for example. In early drafts of the novel, the story began well before the epidemic started and, as Anderson says, "dragged the waif through all sorts of interesting, but unnecessary, adventures in the city."[29] In her decision to pick up the narrative pace, these scenes were cut. Similarly,

Anderson experimented with her portrayal of Mattie's mother, first imagining her as Mattie's aunt. She realized, however, "that Mattie's journey was meant to be a hard one, and the stakes had to be high."[30] The mother's contraction of the disease was painful but necessary.

Anderson tinkered, too, with the novel's point of view. She initially wrote in the third person, feeling that writing in the first person was an arrogant assumption that she could somehow speak authentically in the voice of someone not of her time. Her opinion changed in the process of drafting, however, as she realized, "Unless I know my characters and their world intimately enough to write in the first person, I had no business trying to tell their story."[31] Capturing the voices of these historical characters proved tricky, as well. Anderson wavered between the desire to create authentic dialogue and dialogue likely to be understood by her teen readers. Although the decision proved difficult, she opted for readability, concluding that readers would not enjoy the story if they had to struggle through the language. To maintain some sense of linguistic accuracy, Anderson infused the novel with speech patterns and slang commonly used in 1793.[32]

There was a particular scene that Anderson felt compelled to omit because it proved to be just too real for her intended readers. She shared an early section of the book with the children in her daughter's fifth grade classroom, namely a scene describing the bleeding process as a means to help the fictional mother heal. As Anderson reports, the scene was "pretty detailed. And I read it out loud. And the room was warm. It was after lunchtime. And a little girl in the back of the room went [fainting noise] and passed right out cold."[33] As a mother, Anderson was concerned about the welfare of the child. "But this little part of me—the writer part—," she admits, "was like, 'I did it!'"[34] In the end, she decided to remove the scene to avoid any other similar reader responses.

OTHER ITERATIONS OF THE NOVEL

Several readers have requested that Anderson write a sequel to the novel. Many are especially curious about what will happen between Mattie and Nathaniel. Anderson says she has considered writing the next steps in Mattie's story but hasn't made any final determination as of yet. She promises, however, that if she does write a sequel, "Mattie and Nathaniel will definitely get married."[35]

The novel has also been rewritten as a stage play that premiered in May 2004 at the Gifford Family Theatre in Syracuse, New York. Steve Braddock, the same writer and director responsible for the stage version of *Speak*, adapted the novel and served as the play's director. This alternate version of *Fever 1793* won the Best New Original Play Award from SALT, the Syracuse Area Live Theater group.

CLASSROOM POPULARITY

Given the novel's connections to the American history curriculum taught in many schools and the opportunity for historical bridging that it provides, *Fever 1793* has proven particularly popular among middle and high school teachers. To accommodate attempts to incorporate the novel into the classroom setting, Anderson includes teacher resources on her author Web site.[36] In addition to listing suggested discussion questions and activities generated by classroom teachers, the site also includes suggestions for interdisciplinary teaching and references to primary source documents students might find useful in their attempts to better understand the events of this time, including some of those used by Anderson in her own research.

NOTES

1. *Philadelphia Inquirer*, 2000, www.writerlady.com/fever1793_reviews.html.
2. *New York Times Upfront*, 13 November 2000.
3. Patty Campbell, *Amazon.com* Review, www.amazon.com.
4. Stefani Koorey, *Voice of Youth Advocates* (December 2000): 344.
5. Constance Decker Thompson, *New York Times Book Review*, 19 November 2000, 45.
6. Kathleen Isaacs, *School Library Journal* (August 2000): 177.
7. *Kirkus Reviews*, 15 June 2000.
8. Thompson, 45.
9. Isaacs, 177.
10. Kathleen Karr, *Children's Literature*, 2000, http://childrenslit.com.
11. Campbell.
12. Paula Rohrlick, *Kliatt*, 1 March 2002.
13. Stephanie Zvirin, *Booklist*, 15 December 2001, 728.

14. Isaacs, 177.

15. Karr.

16. Frances Bradburn, *Booklist*, 1 October 2000, 332.

17. *Publishers Weekly*, 31 July 2000, 96.

18. Anita L. Burkam, *Horn Book Magazine* 76, no. 5 (2000): 562–63.

19. Laurie Halse Anderson, "Frequently Asked Questions," *Author Website*, www.writerlady.com/faqh.html.

20. Christine M. Hill, "Laurie Halse Anderson Speaks: An Interview," *Voice of Youth Advocates* 23, no. 5 (2000): 325–27.

21. Laurie Halse Anderson, "Up for Discussion—The Writing of *Fever 1793*: A Historical Detective Searches for the Truth," *School Library Journal*, 1 May 2001.

22. Laurie Halse Anderson, "Live Journal," 24 May 2005, http://halseanderson.livejournal.com.

23. Laurie Halse Anderson, "Live Journal," 19 December 2004, http://halseanderson.livejournal.com.

24. Anderson, "Live Journal," 19 December 2004.

25. Anderson, "Up for Discussion."

26. Laurie Halse Anderson, *Fever 1793* (New York: Simon and Schuster, 2000), 1.

27. Anderson, *Fever 1793*, 24.

28. Anderson, *Fever 1793*, 178.

29. Anderson, "Up for Discussion."

30. Anderson, "Up for Discussion."

31. Anderson, "Up for Discussion."

32. Anderson, "Up for Discussion."

33. "A Video Interview with Laurie Halse Anderson," *Adolescent Literacy*, 2009, www.adlit.org/transcript_display/28150.

34. "A Video Interview with Laurie Halse Anderson."

35. Anderson, "Frequently Asked Questions."

36. See www.writerlady.com/novelsh/f_guide.html.

Chapter Five

———————O———————

Catalyst

ANDERSON RETURNED TO contemporary times in her next novel. *Catalyst* (2002) centers on Kate Malone, an eighteen-year-old Advanced Placement chemistry student and cross-country runner whose primary goal in life is to gain entrance into the Massachusetts Institute of Technology (MIT), her deceased mother's alma mater and the only college to which she applies. Kate's clergyman father pays more attention to members of his flock than to his own daughter and son. As Kate awaits the acceptance letter that will afford her escape from her emotionally absent father and physically absent mother, she runs. Night after night, she seeks solace under a cloak of darkness that allows her to temporarily forget her frustrations and fears as she finds her stride and moves like a machine. Her planned escape is thwarted, however, when her application to MIT is declined. Unwilling to face this reality, Kate tells no one and instead allows the turmoil she feels to fester under the surface.

Her life becomes increasingly complicated with the arrival of Teri Litch, a classmate and bully, and Teri's younger brother, Mikey. When their house burns down, Kate's father invites them into his home while he attempts to mobilize the community to help them rebuild. Kate slowly begins to understand Teri's anger and put her own troubles in perspective. Her real learning happens, however, when Mikey dies in a tragic accident and Kate realizes that he was actually Teri's son, the result of a rape committed by Teri's abusive father. In response, Kate determines to put college on hold and remain home to help Teri recover.

Reviewer Response

Catalyst was well received by readers and booksellers. At the national level, the novel was named an American Library Association Best Book for Young Adults, was among the American Library Association Top 10 Best Books for Young Adults, and was a New York Public Library Book for the Teen Age. Among booksellers, the novel was included on the BookSense Top Ten Bestseller List and named a Barnes & Noble Best Teen Book of 2002 and a Borders 2002 Original Voices Finalist. (See the appendix for other awards and award nominations for this title.)

Although professional reviewers expressed some disappointment in the novel, they were generally enthusiastic. Almost all praised Anderson for the creation of a believable character who experiences believable struggles, describing the novel as "a deftly fashioned character study of a seldom explored subject in YA fiction: the type-A adolescent. Teens will identify (if not exactly sympathize) with prickly Kate instantly, and be shocked or perhaps secretly pleased to discover that life is no easier for the honor roll student than it is for the outcast."[1] Other reviewers claimed that the greatest strength of the novel resides in Anderson's ability to convey "Kate's anxieties and her concomitant insomnia" and pepper the narrative with "evidence of Kate's sharp humor."[2] The *Kirkus Review* extended this praise, arguing, "the first-person voice is gripping, with the reader feeling as though she's crouching inside Kate's head."[3]

Reviewers also found Anderson's ability to capture and convey the reality of teenage life effective. One reviewer described Anderson as "a gifted writer" who "makes the complex worlds of teenage girls real to the reader, from the competitiveness and casual cruelty of high school to the wisecracks between friends to the families struggling to connect. These are often brutal worlds, raw with pain, but her feisty characters work at triumphing over their setbacks."[4] Said another, Anderson "gives us realistic internal battles that all teens can identify with. The need to be number one, popular. The desire to please everyone, at the risk of not pleasing oneself."[5] A third claimed that although young adult authors often use an unlikely friendship as a catalyst for change, Anderson's "take on human relations succeeds through her fresh writing and exceptional characterization."[6]

Reviewers, too, praised the unique format of the novel. They cited the clever use of chemical titles and subtitles to divide chapters,[7] arguing that these scientific terms and safety tips "anticipate the introspective reactions"[8] and "make intriguing connections to the world of chemistry."[9] Another reviewer cited the work as reflective of Anderson's "eminently readable style."[10]

Given *Speak*'s stellar success, comparison across texts is inevitable—and perhaps resulted in less favorable commentary on *Catalyst*. Reviewers were divided in how well Anderson's second contemporary novel for teens lived up to their expectations, given the effectiveness of the first. A *Kirkus* reviewer held the novels on an equal plane, calling *Catalyst* "intelligently written with multi-dimensional characters that replay in one's mind" and a "complex, contemporary story that carries much of the intensity and harshness of *Speak*."[11] In stark contrast, another reviewer argued, "There is too much happening too fast and readers are left with many unanswered questions, and an ending that seems neat but unlikely. This title has a good premise and some moments of fine writing, but it lacks the depth of characterization that made *Speak* so compelling."[12]

The most consistent critique of the novel centered on reviewer claims that the novel borders on melodrama and results in character relationships that lack depth. "Kate's relationships with others remain hazy," argued some critics. "While this seems to reflect Kate's state of mind, since she slowly shuts everyone out as her MIT-less fate becomes clear, her detachment may create a similar effect for readers." This disconnect, they argued, becomes most problematic in the relationship dynamics between Kate and Teri; once their lives cross, the "action escalates to the point of melodrama." Despite the reconciliation between Kate and Teri, "the underlying changes in the individuals that lead up to this event remain unclear."[13] Ilene Cooper of *Booklist* called the first part of the book "involving and incisive" and the rest "melodrama" that results in a loss of identity among Kate and Teri. "Readers involved with the articulate, witty Kate," she continued, "may find Teri an intrusion, and reasons to sympathize with Teri are often too subtle."[14]

PERSONAL AND SOCIAL ROOTS OF THE NOVEL

Anderson was motivated to write Kate's story for two reasons. First, she wanted to write about a character whose view of the world differs from her own, "about a kid who looks like she has it all together."[15] We admire such young people, she says, even "envy them [and] wish our lives were that orderly." Anderson wished to dig deeper, however, and expose the truth that, "under the surface, they are in pain, too."[16]

Second, she wanted to address the frustration she feels regarding the unwarranted and overwhelming pressure placed on gifted kids in the pursuit of academic success, "often at the expense of their souls."[17] "Our culture," she insists, "has deluded itself into believing that the only road to success leads through a top tier college, preferably Ivy League."[18] For Anderson, success means being "a kind, moral, hard-working person who, in a small way, leaves the world a better place," an achievement that may or may not require a college degree.[19] She is particularly irritated by the pervasive marginalization of young people who choose not to attend college. At the end of high school, these students, argues Anderson, feel as though they have "failed us because they didn't get into a school that looks good on a bumper sticker" when, in fact, "we have failed them. Every teenager in America deserves the chance to explore her passions, stretch her mind, and prepare for the next stage of her life without being made to feel stupid or unworthy."[20]

Anderson, however, isn't advocating that students give up on college. Instead, she wants our culture to "be more honest about the reasons we go to college, and what we hope to get out of the experience."[21] In an essay addressed to teens and posted on her author Web site, Anderson argues that getting a college degree results in additional income and opportunities. "While money won't buy you happiness," she says, "having career options because you went to college will make life easier. It is hard to get by in America without some kind of post-secondary education."[22] She encourages students to take ownership of their futures and make decisions explicitly rather than being pushed along by parents or school counselors or pulled along by peers and friends. She tells them: "Know what you want to get out of your college experience. If you aren't sure why you are going to college, then it is time for some soul-searching and research." Anderson is adamant, too, that getting students into college is not enough; they also need to stay there and complete their studies. She insists, "If you get to college and you don't like it, then speak up. Be strong enough to ask for help" and, if need be, transfer to another institution. Most importantly, she reminds teens like Kate Malone that "college is a step on your journey, but it is not the final station, not by a long shot."

WRITING THE NOVEL

In order to convincingly portray a character both knowledgeable and passionate about chemistry, Anderson had to hit the books and continue her education beyond the walls of a school building or college campus. Although Anderson studied chemistry in high school, she loathed it. To garner what she needed to know to be familiar with the vocabulary and experiments Kate conducted, she immersed herself in the process of learning the necessary content, reviewing textbooks and teaching herself the subject.[23]

One night, in the midst of writing *Catalyst* and concerned about the plot, Anderson went to bed in tears, fearing she might have to call her editor the next morning and tell her she just couldn't pull this book off. In the exhausted moments between sleep and wakefulness, the last scenes entered her consciousness, "thunk, thunk, thunk." Anderson says it was like "watching someone lay the tiles down on a table." She woke up, turned the computer on, and put the scenes to screen. She suspects that they were likely there all along but were blocked by her anxieties—divorce, fear that the novel wouldn't live up to *Speak*, self-doubt as an author. "If there's anything I'm getting better at as a writer," she says, "it's not over-thinking, getting myself out of the way and letting the story bubble up."

Selecting (and Rethinking) Setting

Anderson set *Catalyst* in the same high school described in *Speak*, but one year later. The novel, in fact, includes cameo appearances by characters that readers might have already come to know, including Melinda Sordino. Anderson says that it was "very nice to be able to show the readers of *Speak* that Melinda is doing well."[24] Not only did Anderson want to revisit this locale to see what Melinda was up to, she also wanted to honor her readers' sense of connection to this place. She received letters from readers around the country who claimed that Merryweather High was a replica of the schools they attended.[25]

These comments aroused a sense of nostalgia in Anderson. However, her initial plans for how the return to this site would unfold didn't come to fruition. She thought, for example, that it might be interesting to re-use some of the teachers who appeared in *Speak* but soon realized that Kate Malone is not the same kind of student as Melinda Sordino. Their perspectives on teachers like Mr. Neck, for example, differed considerably. As a result, Anderson decided to keep these teachers in the lounge rather than on the page.[26]

Generating (and Finding) Symbolic Meaning

Anderson uses symbol with intention—and without. She is careful, for example, in the selection of names for her characters, attempting to amuse herself, give English teachers something to ponder, and enhance the story for her teen readers. She attempts to "layer things into the names" so that a reader who cares about such elements will "get a charge," while readers "who don't care about those things or who aren't there in their reading" won't be negatively affected in their ability to enjoy the story. In *Catalyst*, Anderson wanted *Kate* to sound sharp, like the "way a log, a piece of wood, sounds when you're splitting it with an axe." Kate's last name, *Malone*, was selected for its inclusion of the smaller words *alone* and *ma*, and the way they emphasize Kate's longing for her mother.

Teri Litch's name carries similar weight, with *Teri* suggesting images of tearing, and the androgynous nature of the name highlighting the sexual abuse suffered at the hands of her father. And Mitchell Pangborn's last name contains the word *pang*, suggesting sadness, while the first three letters of his first name hold particular resonance to Kate's situation in the novel. Anderson argues that "kids don't have to actively crack this code" while they're reading. If a writer has done her work well, these meanings are made at the subconscious level, too, thus adding enjoyment to the experience.

Similarly, Anderson carefully crafted the symbol of the watch. "Time," she says, is "fluid in the book. Teri and Kate both have all the time in the world ahead of them, but they also have no time at all. The watch was a gift from Kate's mom, and Teri steals it because she wanted a piece of Kate's life. It comes back to Kate stretched out from Teri's large arm."[27]

In contrast, Anderson didn't realize the symbolic import of Kate's donut choices until an interviewer shared her own interpretation. In her initial response, Anderson claimed, "Sometimes a donut is just a donut." Upon further contemplation, however, she scratched her head and suggested that perhaps "Kate's early choice of plain instead of glazed says something about her disciplined attitude toward life, and her move to glazed later is another sign of her opening up."[28]

Charting Character Relationships

To foster the development of her protagonist over the course of the novel, Anderson paid particular attention to the ways in which her secondary characters interact with Kate and prod her in certain directions. Although their story is compelling and emotionally poignant, she chose not to dig too deeply into the story of Teri and Mikey to avoid distraction from Kate's tale. Instead, Teri serves as the catalytic force that inspires Kate to identify the changes she needs to make in her life. As Kate develops a sense of empathy for Teri, she comes to understand that "there is more to life than SAT scores."[29]

Kate's brother, Toby, also prods her, this time in the insistence that she face her past despite the pain it will likely invoke. In one of the final scenes in which Toby and Kate stand together in the kitchen, Anderson describes their dialogue as "artificial" and says readers must recognize and analyze the "surface action" of the characters to determine "what they are really feeling."[30] In this case, the tension between "what they say and what they feel grows until Kate snaps and the tableaux of family life, the ephemera on the fridge, all falls down." While Toby attempts to convince Kate to open up, she throws herself into the process of covering, wrapping, and boxing the remaining food—"precisely what she is trying to do with her feelings." Toby serves as the antithesis, "gobbling cake, feeding himself, trying to absorb everything he can so he can grow into manhood."

Kate's rocky relationship with her father spurs her desire to escape. Because he immerses himself in a role that takes him away from his family, perhaps seeking his own form of escape, unwittingly or otherwise, he pushes her away. Anderson needed this tension to allow Kate to grow as a character, but she would have liked to see Kate "turn off the phones and sit her father down and tell him exactly how she feels and what she needs."[31] In response, she would hope Kate's father would "buy a clue and look at the problems in his own house instead of rushing out to solve the ills of the world."

Anderson sees herself in several of these characters. Due to their shared role of preacher's daughter, she identifies with Kate. She also shares Kate's friend Travis's "healthy view" of life despite how hard he has to work. Her connection to Teri, however, is "harder to define, deeper, more raw," even "angry."[32] Anderson expresses love for Teri's character—even though she fears many readers don't particularly like her. She says that someday she'll further explore Teri's story, but when she does, it will result in a book that she writes for herself. If it gets published, great; if not, that's okay, too. "I want that to be one of those books that I write without thinking about anybody else except just the story."

THE FINISHING TOUCH

Anderson generated over fifty possible titles before settling on *Catalyst*, a decision determined more by serendipity than explicit choice. Anderson and her editor were sitting together in a workshop during a conference. Anderson doodled and jotted down ideas—each of which her editor rejected with the shake of her head. Anderson vetoed her editor's suggestions in turn. When her editor had to step out of the room for a moment, Anderson's mind stumbled upon "Catalyst," and she wrote the word down on a piece of paper. A few moments later, resuming her seat, the editor said quietly that she had realized the ideal title was "Catalyst." Anderson lifted the paper and showed her what she had written. "We both got goosebumps," says Anderson.[33]

Catalyst might not be Anderson's most well-regarded novel, but it fills a niche in the genre in its representation of the over-achieving teen and its exploration of the distinction between achievement and compassion.

NOTES

1. Jennifer Hubert, *Amazon.com* Review, www.amazon.com.
2. Diane Roback, Jennifer M. Brown, Jason Britton, and Jeff Zaleski, *Publishers Weekly*, 22 July 2002, 180.
3. *Kirkus Reviews*, 1 September 2002, 1300.
4. Paula Rohrlick, *Kliatt*, 1 September 2002.
5. Roberta O'Hara, *Teenreads.com*, www.teenreads.com/reviews.
6. Lauren Adams, *Horn Book Magazine* 78, no. 6 (2002): 746.
7. Lynn Bryant, *School Library Journal* (October 2002): 154. See also Rohrlick.
8. *Kirkus Reviews*, 1300.
9. Ilene Cooper, *Booklist*, 15 September 2002, 222.
10. Adams, 746.
11. *Kirkus Reviews*, 1300.
12. Bryant, 154.

13. Roback, Brown, Britton, and Zaleski, 180.

14. Cooper, 222.

15. Debbi Michiko Florence, "An Interview with Children's Author Laurie Halse Anderson," http://www.debbimichikoflorence.com.

16. Florence, "An Interview with Children's Author Laurie Halse Anderson."

17. "Laurie Halse Anderson Chats with Readergirlz," *Readergirlz*, 23 June 2008, www.mitaliblog.com/search/label/Author%20Interviews.

18. Laurie Halse Anderson, "Live Journal," 6 December 2005, http://halse anderson.livejournal.com.

19. Anderson, "Live Journal," 6 December 2005.

20. Florence, "An Interview with Children's Author Laurie Halse Anderson."

21. Laurie Halse Anderson, "Live Journal," 17 December 2004, http://halseanderson.livejournal.com.

22. Laurie Halse Anderson, "College Peasure Essay: What Your Guidance Counselor Didn't Tell You . . . and Your Parents Don't Know," *Author Website*, www.writerlady.com/novelsh/c_essay.html.

23. Florence, "An Interview with Children's Author Laurie Halse Anderson."

24. Little Willow, "Interview: Laurie Halse Anderson," *Slayground*, 5 August 2007, http://slayground.livejournal.com.

25. Florence, "An Interview with Children's Author Laurie Halse Anderson."

26. Little Willow, "Interview: Laurie Halse Anderson."

27. Holly Atkins, "An Interview with Laurie Halse Anderson," *St. Petersburg Times: Tampa Bay*, 15 December 2003, www.sptimes.com.

28. Atkins, "An Interview with Laurie Halse Anderson."

29. Anderson, "Live Journal," 6 December 2005.

30. Atkins, "An Interview with Laurie Halse Anderson."

31. Florence, "An Interview with Children's Author Laurie Halse Anderson."

32. Laurie Halse Anderson, "Live Journal," 19 March 2008, http://halseanderson.livejournal.com.

33. Florence, "An Interview with Children's Author Laurie Halse Anderson."

Chapter Six

―――――――――――◯―――――――――――

Prom

ON THE ACKNOWLEDGMENTS PAGE of *Prom* (2005), her third contemporary novel for teens, Anderson sends a "loud, rowdy shout-out to all the 'normal' kids" who talked to her over the years and told her "nobody ever writes about them."[1] Set in a working-class Philadelphia neighborhood and featuring characters rich in "yo's" and "youse," *Prom* describes a demographic not often found in young adult fiction.

THE STORY

Eighteen-year-old Ashley Hannigan, the novel's protagonist, wants nothing more than her senior year to end so she can finally move into an apartment with her boyfriend, T.J., a high school drop-out with a reputation for trouble. Living with him, she assumes, would certainly be better than living in her parents' basement and having to deal with her three annoying brothers, goofy father, and very pregnant mother who serves as a repulsive reminder that her parents have sex.

Ashley's disinterest in school extends to the prom, an event she describes as "stupid" despite the fact that her girlfriends are all counting on this to be the night of nights.[2] Her best friend, Nat, prom-planning committee chair, is devastated when the school community learns that the event will likely be cancelled because the faculty advisor, a new math teacher, stole the prom funds to pay off her college loans. Wanting to console her friend, Ashley poses an alternate plan that just might save the prom and becomes increasingly involved in trying to pull off the seemingly impossible. In the process, Ashley surprises herself with her resourcefulness, strength, and potential—and finds herself caught up in the magic of what she once saw as just a dance. Her chance to see the result of her efforts is almost dashed, however, when she is denied admission to the prom due to her outstanding detentions and library fines. With the help of her extended family and Nat's eccentric grandmother, she finds a way to don the gown and dance the night away, dumping a prince in the process.

REVIEWER RESPONSE

Prom accrued several honors. It was named an International Reading Association Young Adults' Choice, Junior Library Guild selection, and *New York Times* Bestseller. More locally, it was selected as a Volunteer State Young Adult Book Award (Tennessee) recipient and Tayshas High School Reading List (Texas) title. Among booksellers, the novel received the Bank Street Teen Book Award and was named a BookSense Top Ten Bestseller and a Voice of Youth Advocates Top Shelf Fiction for Middle School Readers title. (See the appendix for other awards and award nominations for this title.)

Professional reviewers found much to praise in the novel. They were particularly impressed by Anderson's ability to craft a comedic tale that contrasts with the weightier contemporary titles for which she was known. Anderson "demonstrates her comedic talent" in the creation of a "warm and witty story," said Patty Campbell.[3] The novel, agreed a *Kirkus* reviewer, is "both screamingly funny and surprisingly tender."[4] Paula Rohrlick offered confirmation in her claim that Anderson "has concocted a delightful confection here, full of laughs, warmth, and teenage dialog so true to life you might have heard it in the hall on the way to math class."[5]

Reviewers celebrated, too, the introduction of an often ignored demographic into the field of young adult literature.[6] "Modern teen life just outside Philadelphia is vividly drawn," said one reviewer.[7] Argued another: "Ashley represents a point of view not often seen in literature for young people, that of the kid who's not expecting or desiring to go to college, who's satisfied with her working-class surroundings and future. Her cheerful pell-mell family and neighborhood is depicted with tenderness as well as humor."[8]

Reviewers had much to say about Anderson's success in creating a setting rich in realism through the use of quick pacing and sharp dialogue reflective of adolescent discourse patterns. The novel is described as a "light, fast read,"[9] an "energetic" tale that "offers snappy commentary about high-school life."[10] Anderson "keeps the pace swift, dividing the narrative into numbered sections that are more brief scenes than chapters and emphasizing snappy dialogue that's imbued with the reality of long-time friendships."[11] Another reviewer added, "In clipped chapters (some just a sentence long), Ashley tells her story in an authentic, sympathetic voice that combines gum-snapping, tell-it-like-it-is humor with honest questions about her future."[12] Anderson "hits the voice of her teen readers dead-on. The language and dialogue used in the story are straight out of the halls from any high school in the country."[13] Ashley's voice, in particular, is described as carrying the story "swiftly along on a current of truth-telling, funny pop-culture references, and true-to-life kidspeak."[14]

Anderson's creation and use of secondary characters in the novel received attention as well. According to one critic, Ashley's mother and Nat's grandmother "jump off the page."[15] Another said that these "memorable" supporting characters add "sparkle,"[16] and a third promised readers that the "humorous antics of quirky characters will add to the fun."[17]

The most consistent praise for the novel, however, came in the form of comments commending Anderson on her talents in crafting a novel likely to appeal to her audience. "Whether or not readers have been infected by prom fever themselves," argued one reviewer, "they will be enraptured and amused by Ashley's attitude-altering, life-changing commitment to a cause."[18] In this "tale about the impulse to have one's moment of celebration," argued another, "readers will revel in Ashley's opportunity while dreaming of their own."[19] "Few adolescent girls will be able to resist Anderson's modern fairy tale."[20]

Reviewers commented specifically on the visceral reaction this story might have on readers, claiming that Anderson "holds a mirror to the average girl's high school experience and reflects some images that will have readers nodding their heads."[21] Another noted, "It's also full of sly throwaway references: oaths taken on a copy of *Lord of the Rings* instead of a Bible, Ash's dad singing Aerosmith, accounts that read, 'he was all . . . I was all . . . then he was all.' Expect teen readers to be quoting aloud to each other, and giggling."[22] One reviewer explained why the novel might have such appeal and response: Anderson "finds humor and heartache in a situation that's pretty ordinary. But that's the key to the book's appeal: how normal it is, and real."[23]

Negative critiques of the novel were limited but centered on two elements: characterization and plot. One reviewer found it difficult to reconcile Ashley's "poor academic performance . . . with her intelligence and ambition."[24] Another agreed, arguing that the major flaw of the novel rests on the premise that "it's hard to believe Ashley is as bad a kid as she might have you believe."[25] This same reviewer also found T.J. to be "a stereotypical tough boy" and saw Ashley and Nat's other friends as "filler." The review ended, however, with the comment that the "first-person narration and the essentially personal nature of the story makes this a flaw that readers will overlook." With respect to plot, a single reviewer called the ending "a bit over the top" but recognized that "teens will love Ashley's clear view of high-school hypocrisies, dating, and the fierce bonds of friendship."[26]

WRITING THE NOVEL

Anderson was spurred to write *Prom* due to her fascination with the event as a "common, secular, coming-of-age ritual."[27] Although she was shoveling manure on a pig farm in Denmark at the time of her own senior prom, Anderson had attended her junior prom and that of her boyfriend who attended another school. Like Ashley, however, she was not easily excited by proms or pep rallies or school clubs. Anderson says the book reflects her "ambivalence about this bizarre ritual."[28] On the one hand, the prom is an earned celebration; as a reward for surviving high school, teenagers "deserve a chance to dress up and party together, to push beyond the envelope of their daily routines and experiment with dressing up and feeling special." Yet a prom is also overly expensive and often associated with dangerous behaviors, including drinking, drug use, and sex. Anderson suggests that "maybe the attention that teens lavish on the prom tells us that they want more in the way of coming-of-age rituals. They want a public acknowledgment that they have moved from childhood into adulthood."

Exploring a Character

Anderson's desire to create and explore a character from a loving, working-class family also drove her decision to write the novel.[29] She wanted to write about a "normal girl who isn't sure what she wants out of life and doesn't know where to start looking"[30] but has the support of a "fun, loving, wonderful family" whose members defy the stereotypical vision of the working-class family rife with tragedy resulting from limited financial resources.[31] As usual, Anderson listened and responded to her teen readers, in this case those who represented this demographic and complained that they wanted to read about themselves instead of the middle- and upper-class suburban kids who populated the books on the library and classroom shelves.[32]

An Upbeat Tone

Anderson opted to try her hand at comedic writing for several reasons. After writing other novels in which the main characters deal with emotionally weighty issues, Anderson felt the need "to write something that would make her laugh."[33] "It takes a lot out of my soul to spend a year or two writing a book that has dark and troubling issues," she says.[34] Additionally, at the time she wrote the novel, she was engaged to her childhood sweetheart and was "too happy to write a depressing book."[35]

Beyond her personal life, Anderson was frustrated by the pervasive assumption that young adult literature needs to be tragic and full of angst. She wanted to write a story that showed that there was room in the field for fun and laughter.[36]

CONTROVERSY AROUND CHARACTER AND CONTENT

Not everyone saw this title in this same positive, uplifting light. An adult reader representing Mothers4Morals of Cincinnati, Ohio, posted an Amazon.com review that called the book "*morally* bankrupt! *Shocking*!!"[37] She argued that the novel "promotes everything that parents and teachers *do not* want their teenagers to do!! The 'heroine' of the novel disputes authority, sleeps with her boyfriend, gets drunk, stays out late on school nights wandering around downtown, and then passes out condoms to everyone at her high school prom." Citing the cover photo that "would have one believe it is a sweet, off-beat prom story when it really isn't," the mother expresses her shock and moral outrage over the publication of "these things in a book recommended for our youth."

In response, Anderson states that she and this mother likely agree on more than either would imagine. "Neither one of us," she explains, "want to see kids engaging in dangerous sexual practices. We both wish kids could have healthy relationships with adults they respect and can learn from. We both love our kids and want to raise them with a strong sense of morality and dignity. M4M and I could have coffee, and hang out. Honest."[38]

The primary distinction between Anderson and this mother, however, resides in the amount of trust each affords teen readers. Anderson is adamant that Ashley's unhealthy choices fail to make her happy. Her boyfriend is more of a nuisance than a partner; her future is limited. As the story continues, however, Ashley learns and grows and changes, a realization that seems to be lost on the M4M mother, who seeks to shelter rather than educate young people. Anderson speculates, "I wonder if M4M has so little trust in her children that she is afraid if they read a book like *Prom* they will suddenly start copying all of the behaviors? If anything, her kids would probably say 'wow—that's a crappy way to live. I'm sure glad Ash figured out her stuff by the end of the book.'"[39]

THE CINDERELLA STORY—REDEFINED

Anderson intentionally drew on the Cinderella story in the creation of her tale. She chose Ashley's name with care. Nat's grandmother serves as the fairy godmother, providing the dress that allows the girl to attend the ball. And there is a prince, sort of. But Anderson makes the story her own, highlighting the triumph that occurs when Ashley chooses to write her own version of the tale rather than subscribe to the expectations society has set for her.

According to Anderson, "Teenagers often allow themselves to be limited by how the culture sees them. True freedom comes from the realization that it doesn't matter what other people think of you. When you start making decisions based on your internal compass, that's when you come to life."[40] When Ashley, faced with an expected challenge, rises to the occasion in ways she never imagined she could, she is left stronger and thus more free. This same growth is seen in Ashley's decision to walk away from T.J., the young man she assumed to be her prince. In her relationship with T.J., Ashley looked to the model provided by her parents: fall in love as teenagers and commit to this first love. The object of her first love, however, isn't the knight in shining armor she had hoped he might be. According to Anderson, "the world he offers her falls short of her dreams. . . . Ashley realizes that, despite all his good qualities (and his yummy abs), T.J. cannot look beyond his own desires to see what she needs and wants. He is not good enough for her."[41] With its comedic tone and elements, *Prom* provides additional fodder for the claim that Laurie Halse Anderson can write it all—the serious, the historically distanced, and the humorous—with skill and sway.

NOTES

1. Laurie Halse Anderson, *Prom* (New York: Viking, 2005), Acknowledgments.
2. Anderson, *Prom*, 26, 54.
3. Patty Campbell, *Amazon.com* Review, 2005, www.amazon.com.
4. *Kirkus Reviews*, 15 January 2005, 115.
5. Paula Rohrlick, *Kliatt*, 1 March 2005.
6. Stacy Dillon, Jennifer Hubert, and Karyn Silverman, *Booklist*, 1 September 2007, 106.
7. *Kirkus Reviews*, 115.
8. Deborah Stevenson, *Bulletin of the Center for Children's Books* 58, no. 6 (2005).
9. Karyn N. Silverman, *School Library Journal* (February 2005): 132.
10. *Publishers Weekly*, 24 January 2005, 245.
11. Stevenson.
12. Gillian Engberg, *Booklist*, 1–15 January 2005, 852.
13. Kristi Olson, *Teenreads.com*, 2005, www.teenreads.com/reviews.
14. Katie Haegele, *Philadelphia Inquirer*, 2005, www.thelalatheory.com/reviews.html.
15. Silverman, 132.
16. *Publishers Weekly*, 245.
17. Joy Frerichs, *ALAN Review* 33, no. 1 (2005): 42.
18. *Publishers Weekly*, 245.
19. Stevenson.
20. Lauren Adams, *Horn Book Magazine* 81, no. 2 (2005): 196–97.
21. James Blasingame, "Interview with Laurie Halse Anderson," *Journal of Adolescent and Adult Literacy* 49, no. 1 (2005): 71–74.
22. *Kirkus Reviews*, 115.
23. Haegele.

24. Adams, 196–97.
25. Silverman, 132.
26. Engberg, 852.
27. Laurie Halse Anderson, "Frequently Asked Questions," *Author Website*, www.writerlady.com/faqh.html.
28. Blasingame, "Interview with Laurie Halse Anderson," 72–73.
29. "Authors: Interviews: Laurie Halse Anderson," *YA and Kids Books Central*, August 2005, http://yabookscentral.com.
30. Anderson, "Frequently Asked Questions."
31. Laurie Halse Anderson, "Live Journal," 16 February 2006, http://halse anderson.livejournal.com.
32. Anderson, "Live Journal," 16 February 2006.
33. Stephanie Holcomb Anderson, "Officially Long Official Biography of Laurie Halse Anderson," *Author Website*, 2008, www.writerlady.com/bioh.html.
34. Little Willow, "Interview: Laurie Halse Anderson," *Slayground*, 5 August 2007, http://slayground.livejournal.com.
35. Anderson, "Frequently Asked Questions."
36. Little Willow, "Interview: Laurie Halse Anderson."
37. Laurie Halse Anderson, "Live Journal," 20 June 2006, http://halseanderson.livejournal.com.
38. Laurie Halse Anderson, "Live Journal," 3 July 2006, http://halseanderson.livejournal.com.
39. Anderson, "Live Journal," 3 July 2006.
40. Blasingame, "Interview with Laurie Halse Anderson," 72–73.
41. Blasingame, "Interview with Laurie Halse Anderson," 72–73.

Chapter Seven

―――――――――――――――○―――――――――――――――

Twisted

ANDERSON'S FOURTH contemporary novel for teens represents a deviation from her larger body of work in its male protagonist and narrator. During a speech delivered at the 2005 Workshop sponsored by the Assembly on Literature for Adolescents (ALAN) in Pittsburgh, Anderson described the coming-of-age experiences she witnessed in her son and his friends, concluding that the souls of young men may be likened to their feet. They are big and grow quickly but are crammed into shoe space that is increasingly too small.[1] In *Twisted*, Anderson attempts to make sense of this struggle, exploring the interior lives of boys to capture the thoughts that occupy their minds and reflect their heart's true longings.

THE STORY

Twisted is told through the eyes of seventeen-year-old Tyler Miller, a lonely and unnoticed teen who seeks and gains legendary status when he paints graffiti on the exterior of the school as a prank. He is sentenced to probation and a summer of manual labor and returns to school for his senior year with a reputation and a stunning physique. Class beauty Bethany Milbury notices and appreciates Tyler's new identity and begins to flirt with him. This is complicated, however, as Bethany is the sister of Tyler's biggest bully, Chip, and daughter of his father's boss. Tyler's home life is no less messy. His verbally abusive father is concerned with maintaining the family's reputation and sees his son as a potential liability. His demure

81

mother, in the attempt to maintain the façade of the perfect family, self-medicates with a regular regimen of gin and tonics. His younger sister, Hannah, is his only ally within the family.

Tyler seems to be managing his life in and out of school relatively well until Bethany invites him to a party. As events unfold, Tyler becomes increasingly overwhelmed. When he arrives at the party, breaking probation in the process, he finds Bethany drunk. When she attempts to seduce him in one of the upstairs bedrooms, he defies his hormones and does what he knows he should—he tells her no. She takes the rejection as a personal affront, calls him a freak, and stumbles away. The next morning, Tyler learns that someone at the party took risqué photos of Bethany while she was passed out and has posted them online. He is quickly blamed. Over the following weeks, Tyler endures his peers' cruel taunts, his teachers' unwarranted assumptions, and his father's disappointed stares. Eventually, it feels like too much, and Tyler seeks an out. In the novel's pivotal scene, Tyler considers what it means to be a man in a world where few role models exist—and chooses to forge his own way rather than give in and give up.

REVIEWER RESPONSE

Anderson's decision to venture into new writing territory resulted in praise from award committees and reviewers alike. *Twisted* was named an American Library Association Best Book for Young Adults, American Library Association Quick Pick for Young Adults, International Reading Association Top Ten Title, and was listed as one of the New York Public Library Best Books for the Teen Age and a *New York Times* Bestseller. It won the Eliot Rosewater Indiana High School Book Award given by the Indiana Library Foundation and, among booksellers, was selected as an Amazon Editor's Pick for Teens and Borders YA Book Club Pick.

Professional reviewers called the novel "a gripping exploration of what it takes to grow up, really grow up, against the wishes of people and circumstances conspiring to keep you the victim they need you to be."[2] Critics recognized the likely teen appeal, describing the work as a "riveting book for high school students"[3] and one that will "provide an excellent source of both entertainment and serious conversation."[4]

Much reviewer praise centered on Tyler's character and voice. He is described as "a wonderfully funny, moving narrator and, it turns out, an all-around good guy"[5] whose first-person voice is both "humorous" and "compelling."[6] His insights are "most forceful when they excoriate social pretense with caustic sarcasm."[7] Reviewers extolled Anderson's ability to create a believable character grappling with complex and difficult issues. Said one reviewer, "With gripping scenes and a rousing ending, Anderson authentically portrays Tyler's emotional instability as he contemplates darker and darker solutions to his situation."[8] Another added, "There's something very genuine in the portrayal of Tyler's struggle, both as he seeks attention and as he seeks to banish it."[9]

Anderson was praised, too, for remembering her audience in the creation of this character, particularly in the way she "skillfully explores identity and power struggles that all young people will recognize"[10] and provides an example of how young readers might deal with difficulties they face in their own lives. Readers will be "rooting for Tyler as he battles social hierarchies and power structures with integrity and honor."[11] He may not "gain hero status with his peers, but readers will respect his integrity, which outshines his mistakes."[12] Teens will ultimately "rejoice in Tyler's proclamation, 'I'm not the problem here . . . I'm tired of feeling like I am.'"[13]

Reviewers also addressed Anderson's craft as an author, recognizing her ability to create "taut, confident writing" that causes the story "to linger long after the book is set down."[14] Repeatedly, reviewers noticed (and commented positively on) the balance between moments painful and humorous in the novel. The place in the plot where Tyler reaches his crisis point is described as "one of the most poignant and gripping scenes in young adult literature."[15] The scene is also true to Tyler's character as a result of Anderson's "taut pacing" and ability to describe "the small moments . . . that illuminate his emotional anguish."[16] "His pain is sharply realistic, but suicide is an unlikely ending for the smart boy who's toughed it out this far. His decision to fight back is credible."[17]

Although the novel "tackles head-on many of the tough issues facing older teens: alcohol, sex, grades, popularity, honesty, parents, college and more," reviewers argued that it is ultimately "an uplifting book, mainly because of the freshness of Tyler's voice and Anderson's crisp writing and storytelling."[18] Even in the darkness, there are glimmers of light, created in large part through Anderson's "tight, frank writing laced with humor" that "lends a sardonic, erratic edge to Tyler's narration."[19] When it's most necessary, Anderson "masterfully interjects wry humor that always seems to find its mark."[20]

A few reviewers offered negative critiques of the novel but generally couched their concerns in recognition of the story's merits. The dialogue is described as "sometimes slick and clichéd,"[21] occasionally having "the feel of a teen movie."[22] And some characters, the "jerky jocks" and "hard-ass principal,"[23] are seen as stereotypical, even "a little cartoonish"[24] in their presentation. Other supporting characters, however, are identified as "more complex"[25] and possessing characterizations that "ring true."[26]

The most critical review of the novel came from fellow young adult author John Green. From his perspective, *Twisted* fails to meet the standard set by *Speak*: "It charts a less original narrative course, and the resolution is too pat—a happy ending that doesn't quite convince. And Tyler's voice, while believable, does not lodge in one's memory like Melinda's."[27] However, Green goes on to describe the value of Tyler's story, particularly for male readers in the process of determining who they are and who they want to be. "Flaws aside," he argued, "it's the kind of book that some readers, particularly boys, will keep under their beds for years, turning to it again and again for comfort and a sense of solidarity. What Anderson finds in this book is a way to celebrate the urges traditionally associated with male adolescence—for sex, for domination, for power—without glorifying violence or misogyny."[28]

WRITING THE NOVEL

Anderson enjoyed the reprieve she experienced in the process of writing *Prom*, the opportunity to avoid "getting sucked into the well of angst and depression" required in some of her earlier novels.[29] But after hearing too many painful stories from teenage boys, she felt compelled to write about the pressures that they experience. The boys who wrote to her in response to *Speak* shared their confusion, for example, regarding why a girl would be depressed for nine months after being raped. At first, Anderson responded angrily. "I wanted them arrested," she says.[30] But then she realized that she didn't know boys as well as she had thought and, to fill her gap in understanding, made a concerted effort to listen to what they had to say.

Tuning In to the Voices of Boys

In the process of listening to young male readers, Anderson learned that boys can be bullied and are bullies, often lack strong male role models, are confused by girls and how to impress them, and are allowed to express anger ("preferably on the athletic field") but not the full range of emotions.[31] Although Tyler is a fictional character, he is shaped by the conversations Anderson had with hundreds of teenage boys. In response to their words, she crafted a story that she says explores "the themes of a guy's alienation from his dad, a broken family pretending to be happy, and the despair that leads kids to kill themselves."[32] Anderson admits to drawing at least one experience from her own life with boys, however, saying that Tyler's "ability to eat a mixing bowl full of cereal is something I remember from when my husband was a teenager."[33]

As a result of her foray into male narration, Anderson claims she "came away with more respect for men and boys."[34] She also gained an interesting perspective on her own gender. She describes how "liberating" and "freeing" it was, as a woman, to allow herself to think violently. "I had so many teenage boys tell me when they're frustrated, they're irritated, pissed off at people, sometimes they would fantasize about really hurting somebody. . . . As a woman, I haven't done that much, and I liked it."[35] When she describes Tyler's desire to physically harm his father with "one punch, a long slo-mo shot to the soft underbelly of the beast to make him double over, just one punch, my fist so far inside him that the knuckles scrape on his spine,"[36] she finds unexpected power and release in words.

Writing from a male perspective, says Anderson, was difficult at first. "I spent a loooong time talking with guys and asking how the insides of their brains worked, and what they really thought about."[37] Once she developed "a clear understanding about the motivations and quirks of Tyler," the writing process mimicked the experience of writing from a female point of view.[38] This doesn't mean that the process was easy, however, as writing from any character's perspective is hard work.

Struggling with Plot

Anderson remembers the first day she sat down to write Tyler's story, drawing from the rough outlines of characters that had been forming in her head after the publication of *Prom* and during the subsequent book tour. After her daughter left for school, she explains:

> I got out all my notes, sat down, opened the word processing file and . . . nothing.
> Squat. Diddly. No inspiration. No voices. No ideas. All my notes? Worthless.
> Writing can be a scary beast to slay.[39]

Drawing on her earlier experiences with other writings, Anderson stopped staring at the blank screen after two hours, turned off the computer, and went for a walk. After a quarter mile, she says, "the voices kicked in. I could hear him, my Main Character. I saw the bits of the original opening scene I wanted to use, and what bits were misleading and useless." Anderson walked for a few more hours, stopping and jotting down notes when ideas came to her. Upon returning home, she sat down and turned the rough notes into rough chapters. At that point, she felt as though she had "found the door into the story."[40]

Finding the back door that would lead to the novel's conclusion required additional time for deliberation—and a bit of inspiration, too. One night, Anderson went to bed, wrestling with how the dramatic gun scene near the end of the book was developing. The scene was so dramatic that she couldn't figure out how to end it and move to the novel's conclusion. "If I ended the book with that scene," she argues, "most readers would have thrown the book against the wall and cursed my name for all eternity."[41] She woke up the next morning around 5:00 to the thunder and lightning of a storm. As she snuggled back under the covers, she suddenly figured it out: "It has something to do with this photo of a spider I took on the drive up from Florida. This guy was almost as big as my hand. Someone had spray-painted him orange—probably out of sheer terror. He was orange and he was dead, but he was still scary . . . and inspirational."[42] The spider, poised in its web, reminded Anderson of the ties that bind, a motif that became central to the novel and allowed her to bring the conclusion to bear.

Creating a Cast of Secondary Characters

Several characters both act on Tyler and inspire action on his behalf, thus creating a world of interaction and exchange that Tyler must learn to negotiate. In his friend Yoda's family, he finds both support and hope for what is possible. Anderson created this family with clear intent, "wanting to show that there are sane, loving parents in the world, and they tend to raise really good kids and open their homes."[43] In stark contrast, Bethany's family represents a collection of very unhappy people who, "despite all the expensive trimmings in their life, . . . have no clue how to change things."[44]

Bethany, in particular, proved challenging for Anderson—but not for reasons one might expect. Her greatest frustration with Bethany resulted not from her inability to craft the character she had in mind, but from her son's response to this character. Anderson says she hates Bethany—and that it likely shows in the portrayal she created. Her son, however, describes Bethany as "hot" and expressed his disappointment that she and Tyler don't end up together at the novel's conclusion. In response, Anderson says, "I felt like a total failure as an author as I pointed out to my son that Tyler figured out that he wanted and deserved a girl who had more going for her than just being hot. I think he got it. Maybe. But he still wishes Tyler got the girl in the end."[45]

Anderson is proud, however, of the portrayal of Tyler's father and the way in which his story and that of his son overlap and diverge. She is fascinated by the ways in which her subconscious thought crept into the narrative and created connections she hadn't intended. She cites, for instance, the example of the gun, the way Tyler notices that it smells of his father. Anderson says she wasn't very intentional about this but is pleased by the effect now that readers have pointed it out to her. "The father is hollow," she says, and "so broken and in such pain" that he has "absolutely thought about killing himself."[46] Though Tyler and his father share the temptation to escape through violent means, they differ in how they respond to the choice to live. The father, in life, is already dead, while Tyler chooses an alternative to such a hollow existence. He will instead "find his sense of self, his integrity."[47]

Formulating Symbolic Meaning

As one reviewer noted, "Anderson remains a master at formulating small but apt symbols for emotional truths that trigger both thought and identification on the part of readers."[48] Late in the novel, readers witness, for example, Tyler's habit of picking the blisters on his hands to encourage the faster formation of calluses. This process of physical hardening and toughness represents Tyler's readiness to assert himself as a male by facing his pain; he begins to build a resistance to the forces that have harmed him in the past.

Also demonstrative of Tyler's growth is his favorite computer game, Tophet, a metaphorical journey through hell that, more literally, represents his own lived reality. He spends hours online attempting to survive the sixty-six Levels of Torment, but in his final moments of wisdom, he does more than survive. He beats the game—on the screen and in life.

Even Tyler's last name holds weightier meaning than one might recognize on the surface. Because Arthur Miller's *Death of a Salesman* is one of Anderson's favorite works of American literature, she named her protagonist Tyler Miller as a nod to this author and his work. Anderson explains, "Tyler Miller is sort of the literary grandson of Willy Loman. He's coming from a family who has swallowed that consumer culture dream of 'be popular, be rich, buy a lot of stuff and you'll be happy.' And that's an empty dream. And it's the end of Willy. And in Tyler Miller's book, you can see his dad is trying. His dad is doing everything that society is telling him to do and he's miserable. And he's making his family miserable."[49]

Tyler is *tied* up in a series of "ropes and knots and netting and webs and traps." "On the superficial level," says Anderson, "this kid should be a happy kid. His parents are married. They own a nice house in the suburbs. His parents are employed. There are no poverty issues." But, like many of Anderson's readers, Tyler feels trapped. He wonders what is wrong with him and asks, why can't I be happy with this life? Tyler and his nonfictional peers recognize that "it's a very superficial life. . . . That's why they're aching inside themselves and why a lot of our teenagers wind up doing profoundly dangerous and stupid things. They're in pain."

WRITING ABOUT SEX

Twisted is an explicitly sexual book. From the description of Tyler's penis responding in ways he can't control to the bead of water that runs seductively between Bethany's breasts during a car wash, readers are privy to a minefield of forces that trigger sexual arousal in teenage boys every day. Anderson describes this as "an accurate reflection of the kinds of things teenage guys think about. If anything, I toned it down."[50] In response to those who might question her decision to address sex head-on in the novel, she argues, "I don't see how anyone can write about older teens without working in some mention of sexuality. It's a core component of their existence. They don't have to act on it, but they think about making themselves attractive to people that they find attractive. A lot. That's part of being 17 going on 18."[51]

Anderson includes these scenes to not only reflect reality but to educate readers. She describes, for example, the locker room scene in which Yoda is forced to lie face down on a bench while several jocks gather around him and tape his butt cheeks together as a form of ugly humiliation. Anderson argues that this kind of assault occurs too frequently; she wants to help it end.[52] Similarly, Anderson educates female readers about the power they possess when it comes to how they display their bodies. In the novel's opening scene, the members of the female tennis team host a car wash in the school parking lot. Tyler, the school maintenance men with whom he works, and the male patrons melt, drool, wash their glasses to get a better view, and adjust themselves in response to the bikini-clad "angels with ponytails."[53] Anderson explains her rationale: "One of the things I heard over and over from boys (and men) is how distracting it can be when girls are wearing clothes that show off their bodies. This is something that I don't think women and girls totally understand."[54]

RECOMMENDING READERS

Given the violence and sex contained in this story, Anderson determined to begin the novel with a warning. On the page following the dedication, we read, "*Note: This is Not a Book for Children.*" Anderson argues that it is important to "alert book buyers and borrowers about books that are better suited for older readers."[55] She cites the example of the parent of a second-grader who insisted that her child was ready for *Speak* given the fact that she was gifted and reading on a tenth grade level. With respect to *Twisted*, in particular, Anderson says the story is aimed at (and more likely to be understood and appreciated by) readers older than ninth grade.[56]

For readers ready for the message, Anderson hopes *Twisted* will show them "that they are not alone with their darkest thoughts, that most people go through hell, and that it is possible to survive having parents who are clueless jerks. Oh, and that friends are gold."[57]

NOTES

1. Laurie Halse Anderson, "The Mystery and Magic of Story: A Spell That Connects One Heart to Another," *ALAN Review* 34, no. 1 (2006): 5–7.

2. Karen Coats, *Bulletin of the Center for Children's Books* 60, no. 8 (2007): 323.

3. Alice Cary, *Teens Book Page*, www.bookpage.com/0703bp/children/twisted.html.

4. Myrna Marler, *Kliatt*, 1 March 2007.

5. Cary.

6. *Publishers Weekly*, 15 January 2007, 52–53.

7. Coats, 323.

8. Erin Schirota, *School Library Journal* (May 2007): 128.

9. Brian Farrey, *Teenreads.com*, www.teenreads.com/reviews.

10. Gillian Engberg, *Booklist*, 1–15 January 2007, 78.

11. Lauren Adams, *Horn Book Magazine* 83, no. 2 (2007): 191–92.

12. *Publishers Weekly*, 52–53.

13. Schirota, 128.

14. Schirota, 128.

15. *Kirkus Reviews*, 15 February 2007, 167.

16. Engberg, 78.

17. Adams, 191–92.

18. Cary.

19. Joyce Adams Burner, *School Library Journal* (Fall 2007).

20. Farrey.

21. Coats, 323.

22. Engberg, 78.

23. Adams, 191–92.

24. Farrey.

25. Adams, 191–92.

26. Farrey.

27. John Green, *New York Times Book Review*, 3 June 2007, 35.

28. Green, 35.

29. Stephanie Holcomb Anderson, "Officially Long Official Biography of Laurie Halse Anderson," *Author Website*, 2008, www.writerlady.com/bioh.html.

30. Laurie Halse Anderson, "Speaking Truth to Power," speech delivered at the Annual Workshop of the Assembly on Literature for Adolescents, San Antonio, Texas, 15 November 2008.

31. Anderson. "Speaking Truth to Power."

32. Laurie Halse Anderson, "Live Journal," 2 November 2007, http://halseanderson.livejournal.com.

33. Joan F. Kaywell and Stephen Kaywell, "A Conversation with Laurie Halse Anderson," *Journal of Adolescent and Adult Literacy* 52, no. 1 (2008): 78–83.

34. "Laurie Halse Anderson Chats with Readergirlz," *Readergirlz*, 23 June 2008, www.mitaliblog.com/search/label/Author%20Interviews.

35. Ed Spicer, "Interview with Laurie Halse Anderson," *Spicyreads*, 4 June 2008, www.spicyreads.com. See also Laurie Halse Anderson, "Live Journal," 4 June 2008, http://halseanderson.livejournal.com.

36. Laurie Halse Anderson, *Twisted* (New York: Viking, 2007), 55.

37. Little Willow, "Interview: Laurie Halse Anderson," *Slayground*, 5 August 2007, http://slayground.livejournal.com.

38. Little Willow, "Interview: Laurie Halse Anderson."

39. Laurie Halse Anderson, "Live Journal," 9 May 2005, http://halseanderson .livejournal.com.

40. Anderson, "Live Journal," 9 May 2005.

41. Laurie Halse Anderson, "Live Journal," 20 September 2005, http:// halseanderson.livejournal.com.

42. Anderson, "Live Journal," 20 September 2005.

43. Kaywell and Kaywell, "A Conversation with Laurie Halse Anderson," 78–83.

44. Laurie Halse Anderson, "Live Journal," 27 July 2007, http://halseanderson .livejournal.com.

45. Kaywell and Kaywell, "A Conversation with Laurie Halse Anderson," 78–83.

46. Spicer, "Interview with Laurie Halse Anderson." See also Anderson, "Live Journal," 4 June 2008.

47. Spicer, "Interview with Laurie Halse Anderson." See also Anderson, "Live Journal," 4 June 2008.

48. Coats, 323.

49. "A Video Interview with Laurie Halse Anderson," *Adolescent Literacy*, 2009, www.adlit.org/transcript_display/28150.

50. Anderson, "Live Journal," 27 July 2007.

51. Anderson, "Live Journal," 27 July 2007.

52. Anderson, "Live Journal," 27 July 2007.

53. Anderson, *Twisted*, 2.

54. Kaywell and Kaywell, "A Conversation with Laurie Halse Anderson," 78–83.

55. Laurie Halse Anderson, "Frequently Asked Questions," *Author Website*, www.writerlady.com/faqh.html.

56. Anderson, "Frequently Asked Questions."

57. Anderson, "Frequently Asked Questions."

Chapter Eight

○

Chains

LIKE *FEVER 1793*, Anderson's *Chains* is a work of historical fiction. Set in New York City in 1776 during a siege by British forces against the Patriots, it follows the life of thirteen-year-old Isabel Fitch, a black slave who also serves as the novel's narrator.

THE STORY

At the outset, Isabel and her five-year-old sister, Ruth, live in Rhode Island with their owner, Miss Mary Finch, who teaches the girls to read and write and promises them their freedom upon her death. Their father was sold into slavery several years prior, and their mother dies a year before the novel opens. On the day of the mistress's funeral, an unscrupulous nephew (and heir) appears and orchestrates matters such that the reading of the will is avoided, thus allowing him to sell the girls to the Locktons, a Loyalist couple residing in New York City.

Mrs. Lockton is a particularly brutal owner, and Isabel faces the wrath resulting from Mrs. Lockton's own frustrations over her abusive marriage and inability to maintain the way of life to which she is accustomed. Out of spite, Mrs. Lockton sells Ruth to another family and tells Isabel she has sent the girl to the West Indies, although she is actually still relatively nearby. Mr. Lockton, a sympathizer to the British, meets in secret with other Loyalists and plots to undermine the Patriots' efforts by murdering their leader, George Washington.

93

Seeking a means to secure her and Ruth's rightful freedoms, Isabel follows the advice of a fellow slave, her friend Curzon, and shares information regarding Mr. Lockton's activities with rebel officers. Although she and Ruth are promised safe passage to Rhode Island in return, the Patriot officer later dishonors his promise and demands that she be returned to Mrs. Lockton, who imprisons Isabel and has her branded with an "I" for insolence. Although Isabel despairs the loss of her sister, she distracts herself by doing what she can to provide food and comfort to Curzon, who, as a captured Patriot soldier, wastes away in the local prison. Isabel finds some solace in her relationship with Lady Seymour, Mr. Lockton's aunt, who tries to lessen the sting of Mrs. Lockton's punishments and eventually encourages Isabel to run, to seek the escape she deserves. Isabel realizes that she has no allies in this war. She rescues Curzon and sets out across the river to Jersey in search of her sister.

REVIEWER RESPONSE

Chains has earned several accolades and awards, including some of the most prestigious in the field. It was named a *Publisher's Weekly* Best Book, Amazon Top Ten title, Association for Library Service to Children (ALSC) Notable Book, and Young Adult Library Services Association Best Book for Young Adults. More significantly, the title was awarded the 2009 Scott O'Dell Award for Historical Fiction and named a 2008 National Book Award Finalist.

Reviewers affirmed this praise, calling the book a "gripping novel" that "offers readers a startlingly provocative view of the Revolutionary War,"[1] as well as "excellent historical fiction about a relatively unknown aspect of the American Revolution."[2] Anderson explores "elemental themes of power, freedom, and the sources of human strength in this searing, fascinating story."[3] Another reviewer called the title an "emotionally wrenching and thought-provoking" novel that "knocks on the conscience of a nation . . . tackles America's need for self-reflection, . . . [and] offers a re-examination of history and a new sense of national identity. [The novel dredges] up a past that seems unthinkable to contemporary America, even as it requires readers to think through the many ambiguities that have formed our nation."[4] One reviewer said the novel "vividly captures a chaotic historical time" and provides "a nuanced portrayal of a nation and a girl bound for freedom."⁵ Another found it "historically accurate within an inch of its life" and "infinitely readable."⁶

Reviewers noted repeatedly the depth and quality of historical matter infused into the novel. Anderson "packs so much detail into her evocation of wartime New York City that readers will see the turmoil and confusion of the times."⁷ The story, "well researched and affecting in its presentation," provides readers "a fresh look at the conflict and struggle of a developing nation"⁸ and results in the creation of a "strong sense of time and place" and a "nuanced portrait of slavery and of New York City during the Revolutionary War."⁹ Reviewers praised Anderson for her willingness to present historical details that might make readers uncomfortable, too, noting that Anderson "allows enough filtering and distance for comfortable reading, but expect no holds barred from this accurate author. The times were not pretty, despite the burgeoning of a new America. The writer neither exaggerates nor shields."¹⁰

Anderson is also praised for the inclusion of formal details that lead to a more genuine positioning of the story in its time and place. *Chains*, reviewers argued, is "authentic, right down to the old-fashioned typeface and historical quotes that open each chapter."¹¹ Such details "keep the larger political context before us."¹² And reviewers appreciated the comprehensive question-and-answer section that follows the story and "helps clear up historical misunderstandings and explain this often-overlooked aspect of our country's early history,"¹³ "making clear that imagining Good Americans vs. Bad British is just as simplistic and erroneous as positing Bad American Slave Holders vs. Good British Anti-Slavers."¹⁴

Unlike critical comments generated in response to *Fever 1793*, the reviews identified the perfect union between history and story in *Chains*. In this novel, the history provides the perfect backdrop to a compelling tale, neither overshadowing nor unnecessarily dominating the narrative or characters that chart it. Anderson's "solidly researched exploration of British and Patriot treatment of slaves during a war for freedom" was described as "nuanced and evenhanded, presented in service of a fast-moving, emotionally involving plot,"¹⁵ and the "political complexities of Isabel's dilemma never get in the way of a heart-racing story."¹⁶ The story of Isabel and Ruth remains central, but the novel "brings lively interest to the business of daily life as Washington's army rises."¹⁷ These were difficult times, but we find ourselves wanting to be immersed within them due to Anderson's ability to "temper brutality with a few moments of tenderness and mercy, which, sprinkled like light rain on parched earth, are just enough to offer hope of a fresh start."[18]

Reviewers were particularly complimentary of Anderson's creation of a "remarkable heroine" as the teller of this complex story.[19] As a result of Isabel's "eloquent first-person voice," readers will "care deeply" about her character and the experiences she faces.[20] This is particularly true when we contrast Isabel's generous nature with the selfish emphasis on self-preservation at all costs exhibited by others in her community. According to one reviewer, Anderson accomplishes the "unenviable task of having to write someone in a helpless position who can somehow remain strong in spite of the odds. . . . What makes Isabel such a stunning protagonist and hero is that in spite of the odds and her trials, she is able to look out for other people even in the midst of her own wants and needs."[21] "Far more than history," another argued, "*Chains* is also a portrait of a single young woman struggling to make her way through a social structure that practically guarantees her failure. Isabel's body may be captive, but her spirit and imagination can never be truly enslaved."[22]

Two critics expressed concern over the novel's slower moments. One argued that "the specifics of Isabel's daily drudgery may slow some readers."[23] And another expressed concern that "there are some portions in this book where not a lot happens and you find yourself waiting for the next event to take place."[24] Both note, however, the necessity of these more contemplative passages, the ways in which they "communicate the brutal rhythms of unrelenting toil, helping readers to imagine vividly the realities of Isabel's life."[25] In these moments, "Isabel has to remain a kind of static character"—"she has to bide her time and you, the reader, are biding right alongside her."[26] These comments align well with Anderson's own explanation of this seeming downtime. After her sister is sold and her escape attempt is thwarted, Isabel is "submerged in six months of depression and sorrow."[27] She needs time to mourn before she can move ahead.

WRITING THE NOVEL

In explaining the origins of *Chains*, Anderson argues, "Ben Franklin made me write this book."[28] While researching *Fever 1793*, Anderson uncovered information that shocked her: Benjamin Franklin, her childhood hero, owned slaves, 20 percent of New York City residents in 1776 were held in bondage, and the Revolutionary War wasn't intended to free all Americans.[29]

Storytelling as Sense-Making

Disheartened but curious, Anderson began to learn all she could about slavery in the Colonial period and during the Revolution. At the same time, she was researching and writing *Independent Dames*, a nonfiction picture book about the girls and women who participated in the American Revolution. Anderson explains, "The threads of Colonial slavery and the women and girls of the time period wove together in my heart. The result was *Chains*."[30]

Anderson realized, too, that she had uncovered information not typically taught in history class, information that she argues is essential if America is to "shed the sin of racism." Americans must "come to understand the full history and extent of slavery," something her book might encourage young readers to do.[31]

These ideas were affirmed when Anderson attended an art exhibit in New York City entitled "Slavery in New York." Upon entering, she noticed the shapes of a man and a woman made out of thin wire. "Your eyes could almost go over them and not see them. I thought a lot about what it might have been like to be a person who was enslaved during a time when everyone around you was talking about freedom and liberty—only they weren't talking about you."[32] Anderson wrote the book, in part, to understand how her country could fight a war for freedom but still allow so many of its people to remain in bondage.[33]

Fiction as (Re)vision of Historical Understanding

Writing historical fiction often yields a more complex portrayal of historical events than history books or feature films. The result often offers contradictions to what we think we know about what happened then. Writing historical fiction might be seen as a political act, one that uncovers and conveys versions of truth that readers might struggle to hear and accept. As Anderson says, "It's hard for us to look back on the colonial time period because we're so used to celebrating the Revolution and liberty and freedom."[34] But the truth is that "half of the signers of the Declaration of Independence and a third of the members of the Continental Congress owned people; they had the opportunity in the writing of the Constitution to free all Americans and extend those liberties to all Americans, and they didn't. They chained our country for a very, very long time with that decision."[35] Although these truths might mar our more romanticized views of our founding fathers, they represent necessary knowledge in the pursuit of real liberty for all.

In her writing of historical fiction, Anderson tries to understand the events that unfolded "both in the context of their own time period and through our modern lens."[36] In *Chains*, Anderson achieves this dual purpose by juxtaposing the words of the past with a story for those of our time. Each chapter begins with quotations taken from historical documents of the period: excerpts from political tracts, including Thomas Paine's *Common Sense*; letters such as those from Abigail Adams to her husband, John Adams; advertisements offering monies for the return of escaped slaves; and handbills, summonses, newspaper articles, and journal entries. One critic claims that these quotations provide a counternarrative that allows us "to place Isabel's dilemma, and the dilemma of all the New York slaves of this time period, in history. Thus does Anderson give everyone a voice without sacrificing that of her main character."[37]

Isabel's story also provides a counternarrative to the history reflected in what we've come to accept as truth. Some of these quotations are from voices often unheard, such as a petition for freedom drafted by a group of slaves to Massachusetts Governor Thomas Gage in May 1774.[38] These words remind readers that there are more actors involved than those they study in school, that other voices have been silenced in the attempt to simplify history, to make it less controversial, less complex, and thus easier to learn.

Other quotations come from Patriot leaders whom young people have been taught to admire, but their words sometimes surprise in the way they contradict our vision of the leader who utters them. At the start of one chapter, for example, Anderson includes Thomas Jefferson's comments on slavery: "But as it is, we have the wolf by the ear, and we can neither hold him, nor safely let him go. Justice is in one scale, and self-preservation in the other."[39] In the narrative that follows, we read of Isabel's imprisonment—the savage beatings she suffers, the cruel humiliation she faces—all acceptable under the rule of law. We can't help but wonder whether the "self-preservation" of which Jefferson speaks comes at too high a price; in light of Isabel's story, "justice" seems the only acceptable recourse.

Similarly, Ben Franklin's words begin another chapter: "Our slaves, sir, cost us money, and we buy them to make money by their labour. If they are sick, they are not only unprofitable, but expensive".[40] In the moments that follow, we learn of Isabel's branding and the melancholy she feels as a result of her physical pain and the emotional suffering she experiences as a result of losing her sister. She is sick at heart and, if we ascribe to Franklin's words, unworthy of her price.

The Challenge of Speaking on Another's Behalf

Anderson argues that the most pressing challenge of writing this novel was determining whether or not it was her story to tell, particularly as a white woman who, as a member of the dominant culture, benefits from the color of her skin.[41] Anderson attributes her ability to work through this tension to conversations shared with her African American editor, Kevin Lewis. Together, they repeatedly discussed issues of race in America and how the country might move forward in light of its racial heritage. Anderson and Lewis came to the conclusion that, if Anderson was unable to "get into the head of a slave, then there was probably no hope for America" and that we might fulfill the dream of the American Revolution through the development of empathy on the part of writers and their readers.[42]

According to Anderson, "This is an American story—our story. I believe that as an artist, I have the obligation and skills to empathize with people of all backgrounds, of all conditions, of all times."[43] In response, readers must learn to "look at things that are uncomfortable, look them full in the eye and say, 'Wow, this is making me squirm. I need to learn more about it, take those lessons and move forward.'"[44]

FROM FRUSTRATION TO HOPE

Although *Chains* was born out of anger and shock about America's past, Anderson, in the process of writing, reached a more hopeful place. She says,

> My melancholy about the poisonous effects of slavery lifted as I understood that people like Isabel and her friend Curzon were the real Americans, the quiet ones who fought battles every day and grew stronger in

the face of resistance. They were willing to risk everything for liberty, knowing that it is better to die fighting than to live in chains. But it is best to live free, in a world where we are all valued, in the world that our Founding Fathers and Mothers dreamed of, even if they weren't brave enough to make the journey in their lifetimes.[45]

Anderson hopes that young readers will find knowledge and understanding in Isabel's story, that they'll be inspired to believe in and fight for liberty and justice for all. This is particularly true given the racism that remains pervasive in American society. "Slavery," argues Anderson, "is the elephant in our country's living room. It won't go away until we acknowledge, understand, and deal with it,"[46] even though the topic might lead to discomfort and "make white people feel bad. The truth of the matter is that this country was built on the backs and in the blood of millions of enslaved people. And that is an uncomfortable truth to ponder."[47] Yet we can only move forward through knowledge and connection and conversation. As Anderson advocates, "We need to learn about slavery to understand how we got here. We need to admit that many people are ignorant of cultures other than their own. We all need to talk to each other, and offer respect instead of assumptions."[48]

THE CONVERSATION CONTINUES

Given Anderson's passion for the topic and commitment to telling these characters' stories, *Chains* will be followed by two other historical young adult titles. Anderson is currently working on *Forge*, a novel that follows Curzon, Isabel's friend and fellow slave, as he continues to fight for the Patriot cause and faces winter at Valley Forge. Anderson expects that the third of the linked novels will address the end of the war, the southern campaign in the Carolinas, Yorktown, and Virginia. She is particularly interested in examining how the ways in which freedom and slavery were addressed at this time set up and shaped the Civil War years later.[49]

Anderson has already immersed herself in the research for *Forge*, traveling to several historical sites that afford her knowledge that will ultimately wind its way into the story. She calls this her "boots on the ground research: visiting sites and bugging the experts for the small details, the real-life stuff that many academic historians don't put in their books but that make scenes come to life for readers."[50] Throughout the process, she is full of questions. When she attended a Revolutionary War encampment and reenactment at Old Sturbridge Village in Sturbridge, Massachusetts, her questions led to a better understanding of how one "fires a flintlock musket in the air, the finer points of cooking in a dutch oven, and the art of rolling paper gunpowder cartridges,"[51] details that help make the fictional narrative feel more compelling and real.

Anderson prides herself on her research, so much so that she's sometimes willing to go head to head with experts in the field. In the writing of *Chains*, Anderson ensured that she was accurate down to the smallest detail. She remembers doing a happy dance when she learned that upper-class women used mouse fur to enhance their eyebrows.[52] In preparing to craft dialogue, Anderson read letters and journals that had nothing to do with the incidents in the novel, but she read them "for language, looking for phrases and words which people in the time period were comfortable using."[53]

Given this dedicated attention to detail, it comes as no surprise that Anderson is ready to do battle over a tidbit of history she wishes to include in *Forge*. She explains, "I spent a good hunk of yesterday marshaling my arguments for a historian who doesn't believe that oxen were used to pull the artillery wagons towards a fort under siege. I'm pretty sure I'm right; he's wavering, but he doesn't seem to have any evidence to back up his concerns."[54] Once the novel is published, we'll witness the outcome of the debate; my money is on Anderson.

NOTES

1. *Publisher's Weekly*, 1 September 2008, 53.
2. Claire Rosser, *Kliatt*, 1 September 2008.
3. Rosser.
4. Enicia Fisher, *Christian Science Monitor*, 2 January 2009.
5. Mary Quattlebaum, *Washington Post*, 30 November 2008.
6. Elizabeth Bird, *School Library Journal*, 4 October 2008.
7. *Publisher's Weekly*, 53.
8. Denise Moore, *School Library Journal* (October 2008): 138.
9. Tanya D. Auger, *Horn Book* 84, no. 6 (2008): 696.
10. Julie M. Prince, *Teensreadtoo*, www.teensreadtoo.com/ChainsAnderson.html.
11. Norah Piehl, *Teenreads.com*, www.teenreads.com/reviews.

12. Mary Harris Russell, *Chicago Tribune*, 25 October 2008.

13. Piehl.

14. Elizabeth Bush, *Bulletin of the Center for Children's Books* 62, no. 3 (2008).

15. *Publisher's Weekly*, 53.

16. Bush.

17. Julie Just, *New York Times Book Review*, 21 December 2008, 13.

18. Fisher.

19. *Kirkus Reviews*, 1 September 2008, 938.

20. *Kirkus Reviews*, 938.

21. Bird.

22. Piehl.

23. Gillian Engberg, *Booklist*, 1 November 2008, 42–43.

24. Bird.

25. Engberg, 42–43.

26. Bird.

27. "2008 National Book Award Finalist, Young People's Literature," *National Book Foundation Interview*, 2008, www.nationalbook.org.

28. Diane Mack, "*Chains* Sees the Revolutionary War through the Eyes of the Young," *National Public Radio*, 13 November 2008, http://www.publicbroadcasting .net.

29. Bird.

30. Laurie Halse Anderson, "Frequently Asked Questions," *Author Website*, www.writerlady.com/faqh.html.

31. "Laurie Halse Anderson 2009 on *Chains*," *Bookfiends Kingdom*, www .bfkbooks.com.

32. Linda M. Castellitto, "Making History Come Alive for Young Readers," *First Person Book Page*, November 2008, www.bookpage.com.

33. "Laurie Halse Anderson 2009 on *Chains*."

34. Mack, "*Chains* Sees the Revolutionary War through the Eyes of the Young."

35. Mack, "*Chains* Sees the Revolutionary War through the Eyes of the Young."

36. Laurie Halse Anderson, "Live Journal," 6 February 2005, http:// halseanderson.livejournal.com.

37. Bird.

38. Laurie Halse Anderson, *Chains* (New York: Simon and Schuster, 2008), 48.

39. Anderson, *Chains*, 141.

40. Anderson, *Chains*, 158.

41. Mack, "*Chains* Sees the Revolutionary War through the Eyes of the Young."

42. Mack, "*Chains* Sees the Revolutionary War through the Eyes of the Young."

43. "Laurie Halse Anderson Chats with Readergirlz," *Readergirlz*, 23 June 2008, www.mitaliblog.com.

44. Castellitto, "Making History Come Alive for Young Readers."

45. Laurie Halse Anderson, "Behind the Book," *Author Website*, www.writerlady.com/novelsh/ch_behind.html.

46. Anderson, "Behind the Book."

47. Laurie Halse Anderson, "Live Journal," 10 April 2007, http://halseanderson.livejournal.com.

48. Anderson, "Live Journal, 10 April 2007.

49. "A Video Interview with Laurie Halse Anderson," *Adolescent Literacy*, 2009, www.adlit.org/transcript_display/28150.

50. Laurie Halse Anderson, "Live Journal," 13 July 2008, http://halseanderson.livejournal.com.

51. Laurie Halse Anderson, "Live Journal," 6 August 2008, http://halseanderson.livejournal.com.

52. Rita Williams-Garcia, "Interview with Laurie Halse Anderson," *National Book Foundation*, 2008, www.nationalbook.org.

53. Laurie Halse Anderson, "Live Journal," 30 January 2006, http://halseanderson.livejournal.com.

54. Laurie Halse Anderson, "Live Journal," 28 July 2008, http://halseanderson.livejournal.com.

Chapter Nine

———————⊙———————

Wintergirls

ACCORDING TO ANDERSON, *Wintergirls* (2009), another contemporary novel for young adults, is about "being haunted by an angry ghost, being lost, feeling frozen and not having an ice pick, being trapped between alive and dead, pain that leads to self-destruction, [and] the possibility of happiness."[1]

THE STORY

The novel centers on eighteen-year-old Lia and opens with the discovery that her former best friend, Cassie, has been found dead and alone in a room in a run-down hotel along the highway. The night before, Cassie had attempted to contact Lia by calling her thirty-three times, but Lia refused to answer and now feels somehow responsible for Cassie's death. Through a series of flashbacks, readers learn that Cassie and Lia shared a secret desire to be the thinnest girls in school. Cassie binged and purged (her death was the result of a ruptured esophagus), and Lia ate just enough to keep the secret from being noticed. Lia's success, however, results in such dramatic weight loss that she passes out at the wheel of her car, thus landing her in a treatment facility for girls and women with eating disorders. Upon her release, she moves in with her often distracted and absent professor father, kind but frustrated stepmother, and lovable eight-year-old stepsister, Emma. Her mother, a workaholic heart surgeon, has little time for her daughter who, according to Lia, has let her down by not living up to her high expectations. Lia, haunted by Cassie's death, resumes her destructive eating behaviors.

Despite her weekly weigh-ins and therapy sessions, Lia employs various methods to disguise her illness: splattering ketchup in the microwave; sewing quarters into the robe she wears while on the scale; setting obstacles at the bottom of the stairs as a warning that someone is coming while she spends hours on the stairclimber in the basement. When the attainment of her goals (95 pounds, then 90, then 85) doesn't yield the satisfaction she seeks, Lia resumes another destructive habit—cutting, or carving thin lines into her hips to seek the release of pain. Troubled by visits from Cassie's ghost, angered that her parents don't really know her, confused by her desire to live and at the same time feeling unworthy of life, Lia spirals downward until she can travel no further. At this point, she faces a choice—join Cassie and sleep forever after or create one of a million new (but potentially challenging) futures.

REVIEWER RESPONSE

A *New York Times* Bestseller and Editor's Choice, *Wintergirls* is well on its way to attaining standout recognition and praise. Reviewers have called the novel a "beautiful, heart-wrenching, and important novel,"[2] a "harrowing story overlaid with a trace of mysticism,"[3] a "fearless, riveting account of a young woman in the grip of a deadly illness,"[4] and "necessary reading for anyone caught in a feedback loop of weight loss as well as any parent unfamiliar with the scripts teens recite so easily to escape from such deadly situations."[5] Readers, one added, will be "absorbed by this gripping tale of grief, anger, and self-torture, and they'll be relieved to see Lia tentatively taking steps back toward wholeness."[6] "If you are a parent," another concluded, "Laurie Halse Anderson's new book just may be the scariest book you will ever read. But if you're a teenage girl, *Wintergirls* may save your life."[7]

Much reviewer praise centered on Anderson's portrayal of Lia and the ways in which her character is drawn as "clearly committed to self-erasure as a measure of self-worth and her damages as medals of honor."[8] The smaller Lia gets, the stronger she feels, and the more frustrated and sad we become. Lia's "guilt, her need to be thin, and her fight for acceptance unravel in an almost poetic stream of consciousness in this startlingly crisp and pitch-perfect first-person narrative."[9] Readers travel "with her on her agonizing journey of inexplicable pain and her attempt to make some sense of her life."[10] In the creation of this journey, Anderson is commended in her ability to describe "Lia's history convincingly and with enviable economy."[11] At times, Lia's "narrow, repetitive mind-set makes her a frustrating narrator. . . . Parts of her story are hurried, telescoped, and this can make it hard for the reader to feel much about what is occurring. Yet the book deepens. . . . As her self-destruction gathers force, the truth emerges; the surface placidity of her life begins to crack."[12]

The story takes us backward and forward in time and results in an intricate portrait of a young woman in pain. This sturdy foundation gives rise to what one reviewer called "riskier elements: subtle references to the myth of Persephone and a crucial plot line involving Cassie's ghost and its appearances to Lia."[13]

Reviewers valued Anderson's unwillingness to write about anorexia in ways we might expect. One reviewer noted that she captures perfectly "the isolation and motivations of the anorexic without ever suggesting that depression and eating disorders are simply things to 'get over,'" and the piece, as a result, "rises far above the standard problem novel."[14] Throughout the novel, there are difficult and often discomforting portrayals of the physical effects of eating disorders on Lia and Cassie. Anderson refuses to "shy away from the deterioration of Lia's body, or descriptions of what caused Cassie's death," for example.[15] As one reviewer warned, "gruesome details of her decomposition will test sensitive readers."[16] Yet Anderson avoids the melodrama and glamorized versions of events so often found in narratives addressing issues of anorexia and bulimia: "vertebrae spiking through skin; calling size zero fat; pasting so-called thinspiration from glossy magazines on their mirrors. Not one glossy magazine, supermodel or celebrity is mentioned in this account of mental and physical struggle. Lia's issues are as complex as they are real and universal."[17]

Additionally, several reviewers commented on Anderson's ability "to capture the peculiar lost quality of American teenagers who, to an outside observer, would appear to have little to complain about. She makes their pain palpable."[18] In the process, she presents a more complicated and real understanding of the disease and whom it might affect. Neither Lia nor Cassie comes from an abusive home; neither struggles in school; neither suffers financial duress. But both experience pain that results in destructive behaviors.[19]

Critics consistently extolled the risks Anderson took in the writing of this novel, rewarding her for trying something new in her craft. Anderson effectively uses "strikethroughs and ellipses to show what thoughts Lia is omitting, resisting or rewriting."[20] The inclusion of "struck-through sentences, incessant repetition, and even blank pages make Lia's inner turmoil tactile"[21] and reflect "her distorted internal logic."[22] Form and function unite in the creation of a textual style that embodies Lia's conflicting states of mind, the "struggle between Lia's healthy self and her anorexic self"; her healthy thoughts are stricken, while her anorexic thoughts "correct" what was originally said.[23] The internal battle comes physically to the page.

WRITING THE NOVEL

Anderson had no intention of writing a book about eating disorders. Given her own history of "some disordered eating habits," this was not a topic she wanted to address.[24] After repeated conversations with her ex-husband's wife, Susan, a pediatrician who specializes in adolescent medicine, she knew such a topic might be important to and for teen readers, but she feared the writing of such a story might hurt too much. "I didn't know if I was strong enough," she says.[25]

Simultaneously, Anderson began receiving a steady flow of letters from teenage girls with eating disorders. She met girls at book events and schools who quietly shared their struggles with body image and food. These girls "wanted to get better, but they couldn't get better. But they didn't really want to get better because everybody said they look really good."[26] When we lose weight in our skinny-obsessed culture, we're rewarded with praise. Anderson argues that, as a result, "these girls perceive themselves as strong, which in a way they are. It's hard to deny yourself food when your body is screaming for it."[27] As Anderson leaned in to listen, she couldn't ignore what she heard.

Finding the Voice and Character

Anderson had determined that she would write the novel and that it would deal with eating disorders well before Lia was formulated in her mind. As with *Twisted*, in which she knew she wanted to write from a male's perspective, she began the process with a significant amount of stumbling around.[28] The novel became real, however, when Anderson heard Lia's voice for the first time. Near the end of the novel, there is a passage in which Lia imagines herself sprawled out on an altar, surrounded by vultures pecking at her body. These were the first words Anderson wrote, the first words uttered by Lia when she showed up in Anderson's head and started talking.[29] Anderson says, "I was like, 'Whooooa. This is something else.' So I kept writing." Although this scene ultimately appears much later in the novel, it serves as the driving force behind the creation of Lia's character. Although Anderson spent ample time checking facts and gathering concrete information from Susan and a psychiatrist who worked at an eating disorder clinic,[30] she placed her trust in Lia. "I had to turn off the intellect and let her tell her story through me," she explains.[31]

Concerns about Readers

Given the nature of the topic, Anderson and her editor worried that some readers might use the novel as a how-to guide to lose weight and garner tricks to fool parents and counselors into thinking all is okay. Their concerns were warranted, as evidenced by an article in the *New York Times* following the publication of the novel that spurred a flurry of online discussion on the topic.[32] Because of their original concerns, Anderson and her editor had two doctors, one a psychiatrist, review the manuscript upon its completion. "They said there is no question this book might trigger someone who's prone to this," Anderson notes, "but they said going in a grocery store and seeing a magazine could trigger it, too."[33] She adds, "the challenge in the book they felt I had met was to show the entire story. There is nothing glamorous or lovely about an eating disorder. It's horror."[34]

To ensure accuracy of content, including the debilitating effects of eating disorders on the body, Anderson interviewed physicians, specialists in clinics, and young people recovering from eating disorders; she also reviewed conversations posted in online communities and forums and drew from her own experiences.[35] Lia's behaviors (denial, lying, etc.), as described by Anderson as a result of this research, might be likened to those demonstrated by addicts—behaviors that have been regularly addressed in novels for teen readers. Anderson's commitment to telling this story arose, in part, from her belief that our society warns teens about the dangers of drugs and alcohol but says little about the potentially deadly effects of eating disorders. The problem, she says, is that "dealing with eating disorders can be harder than dealing with drug addiction because the message that thin equals good is everywhere."[36]

Facing the Demons

Anderson says that *Wintergirls* was the "hardest book" she has written, "emotionally, by a long stretch."[37] She immersed herself so completely into Lia's calorie-obsessed character, that she herself lost ten to fifteen pounds while writing the manuscript.[38] "I had to kind of go into that dark place," she explains. "I had body-image issues my whole life. It made me look at the snakes in my head. I would come down at night—because I write in the loft—and just be shattered."[39] Anderson says that although there is some of herself in Lia's character, particularly in the ways she struggles with body image, Lia's voice is not her own. As Anderson says, Lia "got into me. . . . By the end of the book, I felt like Lia was haunting me, much as Cassie haunts Lia."[40]

In the gathering of research and writing of the novel, Anderson also faced the challenge of looking closely at her own parenting techniques—the forces that influenced her attitudes toward food and how she projected them onto her children. In the process of describing the family dynamic in Lia's life, she was forced to consider this dynamic in her own. In hindsight, Anderson believes her "rail-thin" mother might have qualified for a diagnosis of anorexia. While her mother never intended harm, Anderson says, "I definitely got the message that I was valued based on the number on the scale."[41] As she reflected on interactions with her own daughters as they were growing up, Anderson recognized herself replaying some of those same tendencies. "If I could go back as a mom and redo some of the things I did, I would," she says. "I was kind of puritanical. I would give the message that [certain] kinds of food are 'bad.'"[42]

Examining Parental Expectations

Perhaps due, in part, to Anderson's contemplation of her own parenting while writing the novel, *Wintergirls* includes a rich examination of how unrealistic expectations held by parents can threaten the well-being of their children. Lia is a master of deception who does what she can to paint the image of the healthy, dutiful daughter. She worries that she has let her mother down and wishes her father better understood who she is and what she values. She masks her pain by succeeding at starving herself; this is her self-professed strength. In this capacity, she holds herself to the highest of expectations.

Anderson worries that parents too often set the bar too high, demanding that their children attain the unattainable and not attending to the feelings of failure that result when they can't. Anderson worries that "our culture doesn't allow people to fail. Though failure is human, we've taught our kids what they need to do to make parents look good: Excel. In school, on the field, at a job—but none of these address the issue of the heart and soul."[43] This desire to succeed as a means of impressing Mom and Dad leads to a disconnect in the family relationship such that parents "are so interested in getting the right bumper sticker for the Volvo, they lose sight of who their child is and what's really right for their child."[44] Rather than living through our children, Anderson advocates spending time with them instead. She notes how, in her interactions with teens, they say repeatedly "how much they miss their parents." "Adults always feel like teenagers are trying to pull away from us," she adds, "but they really need us in their lives."[45]

A Need for Seclusion—and Revision

Anderson faced a new challenge in the writing of *Wintergirls*—a demanding schedule in the midst of a demanding story. Due to repeated interruptions—travel obligations, conferences, speeches to write, interview questions to answer, final edits on the historical books, research and planning for the next historical, and the arrival of the winter holidays—Anderson felt herself losing energy and focus and needing a break. Upon the recommendation of her husband, she whisked herself away to a local hotel and gave herself the gift of time and quiet. She says she arrived with a character in her head and left with her story on the page. More importantly, she grew as a writer:

> I am feeling better about being a writer right now than I have for about six years. I spent two very, very long days and nights completely given over to a story. I ate and wrote, went out for more food, wrote some more. Ate a snack, wrote. . . . I fell asleep thinking about the story, I

woke up thinking about the story. I had many instances of unreality, not
sure where I ended and the story began.[46]

Anderson returned to the same site on the day after Christmas and wrote
with equal fervor, finishing the first draft and completing much of the
second.[47]

Writing has both highs and lows. Despite the progress Anderson
made on the manuscript while in seclusion, Lia's developing character
held a few surprises in store. A few weeks after gaining her momentum,
Anderson was stopped short, so much so that she discarded the last third
of the novel, removing it from the story and placing it in a file marked
"Extremely Good Writing in Search of the Right Story."[48] As Anderson
explains,

> the main character announced the need to take a different path than the
> one I chose. While it is utterly terrifying to have no clue how the book is
> going to end, I must admit, it's also kind of fun, like skiing down an icy
> slope on a Black Diamond trail. I might end in an emergency room, but
> then again, I might end up in front of the fire in the lodge regaling the
> crowd with a tale of adventure, sipping a mug of hot cheer. Either way,
> it promises a wild ride.[49]

Narrative Risks—Using Lines and Space

The most impressive and exciting elements of *Wintergirls* are found in the
narrative risks Anderson took while writing it. Throughout the story, for
example, words are crossed out but remain decipherable to readers. This
innovative technique highlights Lia's role as an unreliable narrator having
thoughts she doesn't want to admit to having. As she edits her words and
phrases, she self-censors in the attempt to deny the reality of how she
feels. These strike-outs provide "a critical clue to understanding the main
character's struggles," says Anderson, "the perfect device for an unreliable narrator who cannot be honest with herself."[50] Anderson doesn't take
credit for the technique, noting that she first saw it used on someone's
blog.[51]

In *Wintergirls*, Anderson also effectively employs the use of blank
space in ways she hasn't attempted before. At a critical moment in the
novel, Anderson says she "wants the reader to be horrified."[52] To achieve

the effect, she made the decision to insert two blank pages into the novel, literally forcing the reader to stop in the same way that Lia is stopped at that moment in the narrative.

THE POWER OF MYTH AND TALES

From the start, Anderson knew she wanted to draw from the mythical tradition in the novel, identifying this as "a powerful storytelling technique, especially for young people. Sometimes we can say more if we lean on myth. Or we can leave a longer, lasting impression with our readers."[53]

In *Wintergirls*, Anderson uses the myth of Persephone, the daughter of Zeus and Demeter who, while picking flowers one day, is abducted by Hades, god of the underworld. He demands that she be his bride and refuses to release her from the underworld. Mourning the loss of her daughter, Demeter, goddess of the harvest, refuses to let anything grow on earth, thus creating winter. Zeus intervenes and strikes a deal: Persephone must be returned to her mother if she has not yet tasted the food of the dead. Because she nibbled on some pomegranate seeds, however, the deal has to be modified. Persephone is allowed to spend most of the year with her mother but returns to Hades for a period each year. Each time Persephone returns home, spring begins anew, and the earth blossoms once again. Like Persephone, Lia hibernates. She refuses food and refuses to grow, fearing what might happen if she proceeds. Like Persephone, too, she eventually journeys from the underworld into life.

Anderson also draws on the fairy tale of Sleeping Beauty, the girl who reaches adolescence and falls into a deep sleep, trapped in stasis until someone steps in to save her. The difference in Anderson's version, however, is that Lia learns that her fate rests in her alone.

By drawing on these familiar stories, Anderson embeds connections that enhance meaning. She builds on—and often challenges—the accepted narrative, encouraging readers to reimagine their own versions and consider ones in which the girl survives by saving herself. Anderson believes in her characters and her readers, reminding them through her words of the strength they possess—even when they feel most weak and alone.

NOTES

1. Laurie Halse Anderson, "Live Journal," 5 February 2009, http://halseanderson .livejournal.com.
2. Margaret Cardillo, *Sun Sentinel*, 12 April 2009.
3. *Publishers Weekly*, 26 January 2009, 120–21.
4. Barbara Feinberg, *New York Times Book Review*, 8 May 2009.
5. Daniel Kraus, *Booklist*, 15 December 2008, 51.
6. Deborah Stevenson, *Bulletin of the Center for Children's Books* 62, no. 7 (2009).
7. Sue Corbett, *Miami Herald*, 28 March 2009.
8. Stevenson.
9. Carol A. Edwards, *School Library Journal* (February 2009): 96.
10. Edwards, 96.
11. *Publishers Weekly*, 120–21.
12. Feinberg.
13. *Publishers Weekly*, 120–21.
14. *Kirkus Reviews*, 1 February 2009, 154.
15. Sarah W. Wood, *Teenreads.com*, www.teenreads.com/reviews.
16. Kraus, 51.
17. Cardillo.
18. Sonja Bolle, *Newsday*, 9 April 2009.
19. Corbett.
20. Wood.
21. Kraus, 51.
22. Edwards, 96.
23. Bolle.
24. Laurie Halse Anderson, "Live Journal," 13 March 2009, http://halseanderson .livejournal.com.
25. Jennifer Buehler, "A Conversation with Laurie Halse Anderson," *Read. Write.Think Podcasts and Videos*, 28 February 2009, www.readwritethink.org.
26. "A Video Interview with Laurie Halse Anderson," *Adolescent Literacy*, 2009, www.adlit.org.
27. "Dying on the Inside," *Memphis Parent*, 1 February 2009, www.memphis parent.com.
28. Laura T. Ryan, "More about *Wintergirls* and Laurie Halse Anderson," *Post-Standard*, 27 March 2009, http://blog.syracuse.com/shelflife.
29. Ryan, "More about *Wintergirls* and Laurie Halse Anderson."
30. "A Video Interview with Laurie Halse Anderson."
31. "Dying to Be Thin," *National Public Radio*, 20 March 2009, www.hereand now.org.

32. Tara Parker-Pope, "The Troubling Allure of Eating-Disorder Books," *New York Times Health*, 11 May 2009, http://well.blogs.nytimes.com.

33. Cecelia Goodnow, "Laurie Halse Anderson: It Ain't Easy Being Teen," *Seattle Post-Intelligencer*, 17 March 2009.

34. Julie Just, "Interview with Laurie Halse Anderson," *Inside the New York Times Book Review*, 2009, http://graphics8.nytimes.com/podcasts/2009/05/08/08bookreview.mp3.

35. "Dying to Be Thin."

36. Goodnow, "Laurie Halse Anderson."

37. Laurie Halse Anderson, "Speaking Truth to Power," speech delivered at the Annual Workshop of the Assembly on Literature for Adolescents, San Antonio, Texas, 15 November 2008.

38. Goodnow, "Laurie Halse Anderson."

39. Goodnow, "Laurie Halse Anderson."

40. Susan Wilde, "Talking with Laurie Halse Anderson," *Audiofile Magazine*, April/May 2009, www.audiofilemagazine.com.

41. Goodnow, "Laurie Halse Anderson."

42. Goodnow, "Laurie Halse Anderson."

43. "Dying on the Inside."

44. "Dying to Be Thin."

45. Just, "Interview with Laurie Halse Anderson."

46. Laurie Halse Anderson, "Live Journal," 10 December 2007, http://halseanderson.livejournal.com.

47. Laurie Halse Anderson, "Live Journal," 1 January 2008, http://halseanderson.livejournal.com.

48. Laurie Halse Anderson, "Live Journal," 6 February 2008, http://halseanderson.livejournal.com.

49. Anderson, "Live Journal," 6 February 2008.

50. Wilde, "Talking with Laurie Halse Anderson."

51. Ryan, "More about *Wintergirls* and Laurie Halse Anderson."

52. "Q and A Session," Kepler's Bookstore, Menlo Park, California, 10 April 2009, http://halseanderson.livejournal.com.

53. Ryan, "More about *Wintergirls* and Laurie Halse Anderson." See also Kathleen T. Horning, "Fearless: An Interview with Laurie Halse Anderson," *School Library Journal*, 1 June 2009, www.schoollibraryjournal.com.

Chapter Ten

———————————O———————————

Writings for Children

MANY FANS OF Laurie Halse Anderson's writings for teen readers might be surprised to learn that she not only got her start as a children's book author but has published several fiction and nonfiction books for younger readers. Anderson explains her motivation to write for a younger crowd in this way: "My inner little kid likes to play as much as my inner teen."[1]

PICTURE BOOKS

Ndito Runs

Anderson published her first book, *Ndito Runs* (illustrated by Anita van der Merwe), in 1996. Although the title has been out of print for several years, it was translated into Xhosa, Zulu, Afrikaans, and Lesotho for publication in South Africa. The story features a small girl living in the Kenyan highlands who runs barefoot from her village to her school, dreaming of animals to keep her company along the way. She mimics the behaviors she imagines—galloping like a wildebeest, floating like a gazelle—and feels connected to the natural world in which she lives.

The story arose after Anderson listened to a segment on National Public Radio about Kenyan Olympic marathon runners who grew up running miles each day to get to school and home again, developing skills and stamina in the process.[2] In the book's acknowledgments, Anderson notes, "Most children in the Kenyan highlands grow up running miles each day to get to school, and several have gone on to join the ranks of the fastest runners in the world."³ Anderson was "captivated by a little girl laughing in the background as the NPR reporter conducted his interview" and determined that this was a story worth telling.⁴ To gather the necessary information and maintain her commitment to the integrity of the story, she spoke with headmasters of several Kenyan elementary schools and requested that representatives from the Kenyan embassy read the completed manuscript.

Reviewers were generally positive in their response to the book, calling it a "joyous romp through the Kenyan countryside"⁵ that, through "simple, poetic words," expresses a girl's "exhilaration and her connection with nature and with people."⁶ Some reviewers worried that the text might be "labored" at times and that young readers may "stumble over such muddled similes as 'Ndito springs straight up like a warrior watching cattle.'"⁷ They went on to say, however, that "both narrative and art paint an appealing portrait of an unusually vivacious heroine. Readers are sure to join Ndito in her enthusiasm."⁸ As another reviewer noted, "Even with the increasing number of multicultural titles being published, few have this book's melding of illustration and text."⁹

Turkey Pox

Anderson's second picture book, *Turkey Pox* (illustrated by Dorothy Donohue), was published in 1996 and named a Parents' Choice Honor Book. This fictional story is grounded in Anderson's elder daughter's bout with chickenpox on Thanksgiving Day when she was a child.¹⁰ In the book, young Charity looks forward to spending the Thanksgiving holiday with her grandmother, who is known for her turkey preparation skills. In the haste to leave the house, family members don't notice the spots on Charity's face that have cropped up overnight. During the ride, Charity's younger brother, Fred, begins singing songs about the spots, and the parents, upon realizing the situation, are forced to turn around and head home. Charity is devastated, but her hopes are revived when determined Nana treks to the house, roasted turkey in hand, having hitched a ride from a snowplow driver. In commemoration of the event, family members decorate the turkey with cherries to mimic Charity's face.

Reviewers enjoyed the title, calling it an "unusual holiday story" and "rousing complement" to other titles with a chickenpox motif.¹¹ The story's events are "chronicled with humor, leading to a satisfying ending in which it is revealed how chicken pox becomes 'turkey pox,'"[12] and the "satisfying story and appealing illustrations" make it an ideal choice for "reading aloud."[13]

No Time for Mother's Day

Charity and her family members make a second appearance in Anderson's third picture book, No Time for Mother's Day (illustrated by Dorothy Donohue), published in 1999. Charity is confused about what to give her mother for Mother's Day. As she frets, she witnesses the frantic pace her mother maintains in her attempts to deal with the phones and toaster and microwave and dishwasher and errands on a busy Saturday. That night, Charity awakens with the perfect idea in mind; she realizes that what her mother needs most is a bit of quiet. The next morning, she unplugs the clocks and turns off "everything that beeps or bleeps or buzzes," allowing Mom some much-needed peace.

Critics described the book as "a refreshing story about Mother's Day [that] features a terrifically thoughtful girl who comes up with just the right present."[14] Anderson is commended for her "clever and homey text," and the process through which Charity determines the perfect gift is noted as "subtly conveyed, making the lesson far more powerful."[15] As one reviewer noted, the title's emphasis on the chaos of modern life "and how to make it just a bit simpler should hit close to home."[16]

The Big Cheese of Third Street

Anderson calls The Big Cheese of Third Street (illustrated by David Gordon), published in 2002, "a salute to her adopted hometown of Philadelphia."[17] Young Benny Antonelli is "no bigger than a peanut butter sandwich." An outcast in his community of "bus-sized women," "skyscraper-sized men," and "kids taller than streetlights," Benny is subjected to regular pranks. He is tossed around like a ball, taped to a toy airplane, and pinned to the clothesline along with the family underpants. Benny's escape mechanism is to climb street signs and telephone poles, anything that allows him to rise above his tormenters. At the annual block party, however, Benny is afforded the chance to prove himself in a contest in which the winner must climb a greased pole and retrieve a piece of cheese from the top. He succeeds when others cannot and emerges victorious, the big cheese of Third Street.

Reviewers described Anderson's "urban tall tale" as "a hoot, from her cheeky take on the woes of runt-hood to her pliant use of exaggeration and sassy street talk"[18] and argued that "kids who have ever felt left out or picked on will appreciate this 'bigger-than-life' slice of justice."[19] "It probably won't come as any surprise to children, even very young ones, who the hero turns out to be," said another reviewer, "but a lot of the fun comes in showing just how Benny triumphs."[20] A singular dissenting voice claimed that the "book aims to teach that size doesn't matter and that the little guy can triumph in the end, but the execution is unsuccessful."[21] This critic labeled the book "a disappointing effort from this versatile author," arguing that the "tone of the text is flip and smart-alecky"—and failing to realize the necessity of such a voice for such a character.

The Hair of Zoe Fleefenbacher Goes to School

Anderson's picture book *The Hair of Zoe Fleefenbacher Goes to School* (illustrated by Ard Hoyt) was released in the summer of 2009. Young Zoe's parents love their daughter's untamed tresses. Her kindergarten teacher believes they offer consolation and comfort. Her first grade teacher, however, just doesn't get it. "No wild hair in my class!" she insists. The tale is filled with hair-induced chaos and an eventual solution that results from the cooperation between teacher and student.

The story is dedicated to Anderson's daughter Meredith, who was an ADHD-diagnosed child. Anderson admits, "She was a handful in the classroom, a real handful. I always felt like we should leave tips for her teachers." In the fall of 2009, Meredith began work on the other side of the desk, having graduated from college in May 2009 with a degree in education. Anderson wrote Zoe's story well before Meredith's career ambitions were fulfilled. On a conscious level, she says, she wasn't writing about her daughter at all. When she reread the manuscript, however, she realized that indeed it was her daughter's story, too. But Anderson says the book is also about the responsibilities that teachers have, despite the unrealistic demands put upon them with respect to classroom management and class size, to meet all kids where they are—even if it's not where the teacher happens to be.

FICTIONAL SERIES BOOKS

Anderson has published several fictional series books under two different titles. In 2000, the American Girl Company asked her to write a collection of books featuring five young people who volunteer at a local veterinary clinic. The resulting series was titled *Wild at Heart*. When Mattel purchased American Girl, the company opted to cancel the series. Shortly thereafter, Penguin publishers worked with Anderson to reissue the books with new covers under a new name, *Vet Volunteers*. Anderson has published twelve titles in the new series (see the bibliography for individual titles). In one book, eleven-year-old Maggie fears that the sick puppies brought into her grandmother's clinic have come from a local puppy mill. She and her friends band together to locate the culprit and shut the mill down. In another title, the kids travel to Florida, where they rescue an injured manatee. And in yet another, Maggie's friend Zoe meets and works with a therapy dog recently diagnosed with cancer. Anderson says she receives the "best fan mail in the world about these books. Kids send her pictures and drawings of their pets."[22]

Although these titles are not as widely known or celebrated by reviewers, they have been described as "chapter books sure to please middle readers"[23] and have received several awards, including the Henry Bergh ASPCA Award for Children's Books (*Fight for Life*), Children's Book Council Children's Choice honors (*Say Good-bye*), and IRA Teacher's Choice recognition (*Trapped*). In response to *Fight for Life* (Book One), reviewers noted Anderson's success in creating a first-person narrative that "describes the veterinary procedures in simple language and builds suspense in the key adventure scenes" while also painting a picture of Maggie's "grandmother as a feisty, capable vet that will stick in readers' minds."[24] The book was called "a fast-paced story that kids will like."[25] Similarly, *Homeless* (Book Two) was described as "infused with emotion and information."[26] In a negative review written in response to *Homeless*, one critic argued that "Anderson's entry in this animal-centered series reads like vapid, formulaic fiction" and will "likely satisfy only the most avid fans of animal fiction."[27]

Across the titles in the series, however, reviewers highlighted the appeal of the stories to pet lovers and fans of animal-centered fiction. And they noted the value of the pet care facts and nonfiction information that Anderson includes at the conclusion of each story.[28]

NONFICTION

Saudi Arabia

Anderson entered the world of nonfiction picture books with the publication of *Saudi Arabia* (part of the Globetrotters Club Series), published in 2000. The title provides readers insight into the geography, family and community life, and cultural contributions of the country and its inhabitants. In addition to learning about the desert environment, roles of women and men, and school experiences of Saudi kids, readers are invited to trace a map of the country and color and label key elements as well as practice the Arabic names for family members. The text is supplemented with color photos, maps, suggestions for further reading, and a glossary and index.

In preparation for writing, Anderson read extensively on Islam and used the library at the Saudi Arabian embassy in the United States. She also interviewed the wives of several Saudi diplomats to garner a clearer understanding of the lives of Saudi children. Although Anderson found the experience "valuable and enriching" in the way it allowed her to learn more about Islam, she is "not at all happy with the finished project," given the editors' decision to cut out much of what she wrote.[29] One reviewer had a mixed response, arguing, "There are few books about Middle Eastern countries for this audience, and this one has some good things about it," including an "attractive and engaging format" and "positive" tone.[30] But the reviewer also faulted the text for an oversimplification of content that sometimes "results in some broad generalizations" and avoidance of "controversial issues."

Thank You, Sarah: The Woman Who Saved Thanksgiving

One of Anderson's most well-received picture books, *Thank You, Sarah: The Woman Who Saved Thanksgiving* (illustrated by Matt Faulkner), was published in 2002. The title tells the story of Sarah Josepha Hale, a distant great-aunt of Anderson's, whose relentless letters and thirty-eight years of petitioning presidents to declare Thanksgiving a national holiday eventually resulted in success. Hale, concerned that the holiday wouldn't last due to a lack of agreement on the date in states across the country, persisted in her attempts until President Lincoln declared the fourth Thursday in November a national holiday in 1863. Anderson infuses the story with fun theatrics, including dramatic speech ("*We Almost Lost . . . Thanksgiving!*" spread across an image of concerned diners and hopeful turkeys), a warning pertaining to the story's unlikely hero ("Never underestimate dainty little ladies"), playful language ("When folks started to ignore Thanksgiving, well, that just curdled her gravy"), and an irreverent tone ("You think you know everything about Thanksgiving, don't you?"). The title was well received by awards committees and reviewers alike. At the national level, the book earned the Once Upon a World Children's Book Award and was named a Center for Children's Books Best Book, American Library Association Amelia Bloomer List title, Junior Library Guild selection, and International Reading Association Teachers' Choice book, among others. Additionally, it garnered the Oppenheimer Toy Portfolio Gold Award and was a recommended social studies book by the Public Broadcasting Services' TeacherSource. (See the appendix for other award nominations.)

According to reviewers, Anderson turned a "little-known historical tidbit into a fresh, funny, and inspirational alternative to the standard Thanksgiving stories. . . . Anderson doesn't state the facts; she reveals them, unveils them, and celebrates them, and her text certainly shows that persistence and eloquence can succeed."[31] She gives "an inherently interesting story an extra boost with a terse, amusing text,"[32] achieves a successful balance of "humor and history,"[33] and offers readers "both an indomitable role model and a memorable, often hilarious glimpse into the historical development of this country's common culture."[34] Reviewers across the board commended the inclusion of back matter that is "particularly solid for a picture book."[35] The final pages, titled the "Feast of Facts," include "additional delectable" tidbits,"[36] such as mention of Franklin Delano Roosevelt's attempts to move the holiday up to extend the shopping season and Hale's authorship of "Mary Had a Little Lamb."

Anderson is a self-professed Thanksgiving junkie. When her editor encouraged her to write the story, she jumped at the opportunity. The going was not always easy, however. Information on Sarah Hale was difficult to come by, given the fact that a large collection of her letters, scheduled to be auctioned, burned in a warehouse fire in the early 1900s, thus limiting access to primary sources.[37] In addition, determining how to combine the history of the holiday with the life of Sarah Hale proved challenging. "The early drafts," says Anderson, "were written in that dry, dull, old-fashioned tone. I hated it. I felt like I had killed my story before anyone got the chance to read it."[38] During a meeting one day, she doodled a capital "S" with a shield around it. The image reminded her of Superman and resulted in an epiphany: "Sarah Hale was a superhero."[39] This recognition set the tone for the energetic and important story that resulted.

Independent Dames: What You Never Knew about the Women and Girls of the American Revolution

Although Anderson published *Independent Dames: What You Never Knew About the Women and Girls of the American Revolution* (illustrated by Matt Faulkner) in 2008, the project began in the mid-1990s with her desire to write a book highlighting six obscure heroines of the American Revolution. Anderson says, "Nobody wanted the book. They all sent me form rejections. I had done a fair amount of research and had enormous files stuffed with information, but I realized the idea wasn't going anywhere, so I packed them away in my drawer."[40]

After the success of *Thank You, Sarah: The Woman Who Saved Thanksgiving*, Anderson's editor asked if she might like to explore another historical subject in a collaborative project using the same format and illustrator. She thought of the treasure trove of information in that drawer at home and pitched the concept. The editor liked the idea but recommended that Anderson extend the scope of the book and examine a larger number of women. She obliged by conducting additional research that ultimately led to brief biographies of eighty-nine women and girls—and a contract to proceed.

Given the scope of the project and the amount of information they wanted to include in the book, Anderson and her illustrator decided on a multigenre approach that resulted in four types of writing on each spread—the narrative storyline, a running timeline along the bottom, biographical information for each person, and dialogue bubbles written in contemporary voices. The final draft contains an astonishing 11,000 words. Says Anderson, "I sort of broke the rules about keeping picture books short."[41]

The book opens with the narrator welcoming readers to a school play and posing the question of why there are so few roles for women and girls. On the pages that follow, an alternate story of the Revolutionary War is told in the wonderfully smart and sarcastic voice of the narrator. Cartoonish renderings of eighty-nine women (whites, African Americans, Native

Americans) add to the narrative; their voices are captured in speech bal-
loons, and descriptions of their accomplishments appear in highlighted
framed ovals. Readers meet a wide variety of women and girls who sup-
ported the war effort in multiple ways. Slave poet Phillis Wheatley sent
poems to George Washington. Prudence Wright and Sarah Shattuck
guarded the village when the men fought at Concord and Lexington—and
captured a British spy in the process. And sixteen-year-old Sybil Luding-
ton rode forty miles in the rain to warn of a British attack and round up
members of the militia (Paul Revere rode just sixteen). The book includes
references to women whom readers likely already know (Martha Washington and Abigail Adams), introduces many others who are less familiar,
and debunks some of the myths surrounding women like Molly Pitcher
and Betsy Ross.

Reviewers who offered negative commentary reacted primarily to the
form of the book and their belief that Anderson tried to achieve too much
in too small a space. According to one review, the "attempt to include
females in the pantheon of white men in powdered wigs results in a mile-
wide, inch-deep roll call. Readers must juggle four different narrative elements" making the title "ambitious but flawed."[42] Another reviewer argued
that the "jam-packed, busy presentation overwhelms this otherwise fresh
exploration of women's contributions to the War of Independence."[43] This
critic commended Anderson on the quality of her research, saying she
"sure has done her homework, digging out names and particulars of a
dizzying number of strong women from the expected to the lesser known
working to ensure occupational and ethnic diversity throughout." The
review concluded with the claim, "trimmed down, this would have been
a marvelous alternative to the Dead White Men version of history—but
not as is."

Most reviewers, in contrast, embraced the unique form and rich material contained in the book. One reviewer wrote, "The biographical sketches
are all easy to read and do not burden the reader with unnecessary information. . . . Anderson gives just enough information to interest the reader
and hopefully convince them to research further on their own."[44] Another
echoed this sentiment, stating, "The book contains a tremendous amount
of information, and it has quite a bit going on in it, but the genius of its
set-up is that it never feels heavy or pedantic. Information is doled out in
bite-sized morsels, and kid readers will be free to read as much (or as little)
of the information as they feel up to."[45] A third concluded: "although the

pages are rather busy, Anderson's humor is thoroughly infectious, hooking readers in a heartbeat."[46]

Reviewers noted, too, the educative value of the title for young readers. Anderson's "saucy text challenges the conventionally taught— and incomplete—history of the American Revolution."[47] In the process, Anderson "remedies the dearth of material on some influential, but nearly forgotten 18th-century Independent Dames."[48] As they read the "irreverent but informative" information on these "brassy and brave women,"[49] readers will be "both engaged by and educated about this critical period."[50] According to one reviewer, "No one who encounters this book could ever again think history is dull."[51] In speaking of her goals as a writer of history-oriented works. Anderson says, "I hope that my books will help educate a generation (or two, or three) of American children to value the contributions of *all* the people who contributed to our nation's heritage."[52] These reviews seem to indicate the attainment of this goal.

Anderson really wants kids to learn. As part of her research for this title, she studied the social studies curricula and state standards for elementary and middle school students to know what she could expect them to have been exposed to with respect to the American Revolution.[53] And she really wants them to learn the whole truth. Anderson says that as a children's author, she has to keep truth at the forefront. "If you write historical fiction for grown-ups," she claims, "I am told you have lots of latitude to make stuff up. Not in my world. There are legions of librarians and teachers out there who trust us to present accurate information."[54] Anderson values her role as an educator and strives for truth in everything she writes—for teens and kids alike.

NOTES

1. Laurie Halse Anderson, "Frequently Asked Questions," *Author Website*, www.writerlady.com/faqh.html.

2. Stephanie Holcomb Anderson, "About Me," *Author Website*, 2004, www .writerlady.com/me.html.

3. Laurie Halse Anderson, *Ndito Runs* (New York: Henry Holt, 1996), Ac- knowledgments.

4. Patricia M. Newman, "Who Wrote That? Featuring Laurie Halse Anderson," *California Kids*, March 2005, www.patriciamnewman.com/anderson.html.

5. Tom S. Hurlburt, *School Library Journal* (May 1996): 84.
6. Hazel Rochman, *Booklist*, 15 March 1996, 1268.
7. Elizabeth Devereaux and Diane Roback, *Publishers Weekly*, 18 March 1996, 68.
8. Devereaux and Roback, 68.
9. Hurlburt, 84.
10. S. H. Anderson, "About Me."
11. Lisa Marie Gangemi and Trevelyn E. Jones, *School Library Journal* (October 1996): 84.
12. Sharon White Williams, *Childhood Education* (Winter 1997/1998).
13. Carolyn Phelan, *Booklist*, 1 September 1996, 135.
14. *Kirkus Reviews*, 1 March 1999.
15. *Kirkus Reviews*.
16. Ilene Cooper, *Booklist*, 15 February 1999, 1073.
17. S. H. Anderson, "About Me."
18. Diane Roback, Jennifer M. Brown, Jason Britton, and Jeff Zaleski, *Publishers Weekly*, 19 November 2001, 67.
19. *Kirkus Reviews*, 15 January 2002, 100.
20. Ilene Cooper, *Booklist*, 1 December 2001, 644.
21. Genevieve Gallagher, *School Library Journal* (February 2002): 96.
22. Stephanie Holcomb Anderson, "Officially Long Official Biography of Laurie Halse Anderson," *Author Website*, 2008, www.writerlady.com/bioh.html.
23. Joni Praded, *Animals*, 1 November 2000.
24. Lauren Peterson, *Booklist*, 1 May 2000, 1665.
25. Martha Shaw, *Children's Literature*, 2000, http://childrenslit.com.
26. Nancy Tilly, *Children's Literature*, 2000, http://childrenslit.com.
27. Ronni Krasnow, *School Library Journal* (December 2000): 138.
28. Jennifer Ralston, *School Library Journal* (July 2001): 102. See also Janie Schomberg, *School Library Journal* (July 2000): 100.
29. Laurie Halse Anderson, "Live Journal," 5 October 2005, http://halseanderson .livejournal.com.
30. Carol Johnson Shedd, *School Library Journal* (January 2001): 112.
31. Louise L. Sherman, *School Library Journal* (December 2002): 116.
32. Ilene Cooper, *Booklist*, 15 December 2002, 764.
33. *Publishers Weekly*, 23 September 2002, 26.
34. *Kirkus Reviews*, 1 October 2002, 1462.
35. Cooper, 2002, 764.
36. *Publishers Weekly*, 2002, 26.
37. Anderson, "Frequently Asked Questions."
38. Kelly R. Fineman, "Laurie Halse Anderson," *Writing and Ruminating: One Children's Writer's Journey*, 19 May 2008, http://kellyrfineman.livejournal.com.
39. Fineman, "Laurie Halse Anderson."

40. Laurie Halse Anderson, "Live Journal," 20 July 2008, http://halseanderson.livejournal.com.

41. Fineman, "Laurie Halse Anderson."

42. *Publishers Weekly*, 26 May 2008, 65–66.

43. *Kirkus Reviews*, 15 May 2008, 104.

44. *Thereadingzone*, http://thereadingzone.wordpress.com.

45. Kelly Fineman, "Writing and Ruminating," 17 May 2008, http://kellyrfineman.livejournal.com.

46. Tanya D. Auger, *Horn Book Magazine* 84, no. 5 (2008): 605.

47. Auger, 605.

48. *School Library Journal* (October 2008): 11.

49. Nancy Gilson, *The Columbus Dispatch*, 2 July 2008.

50. Lee Bock, *School Library Journal* (August 2008): 107–8.

51. Regan McMahon, *San Francisco Gate*, 29 June 2008.

52. Fineman, "Laurie Halse Anderson."

53. Fineman, "Laurie Halse Anderson."

54. Laurie Halse Anderson, "Live Journal," 20 June 2006, http://halseanderson.livejournal.com.

Chapter Eleven

─────────────○─────────────

Short Stories
and Poems

IN ADDITION TO WRITING novels, chapter books, and picture books, Anderson has extended her range to include short stories and poems, thus demonstrating her flexibility and diverse talents as an author.

SHORT STORIES

To date, Anderson has published three short stories for teens and children. The first, "Yia-Yia's Dance" (1998), appeared in *Highlights for Children* and was one of Anderson's first published pieces for younger readers. The story describes the life of the narrator's grandmother, who dances "like a smooth, sun-glinting, wind-tossed ribbon."[1] Born in Greece but soon transported with her family across the sea, the young Yia-Yia sways to the sailor's pipe, twirls and whirls to school, and keeps a beat with her toes to make chores go by faster. When she meets the narrator's Papou and falls in love, her feet barely touch the floor during the wedding. When the babies arrive, she high-steps her way throughout the house and while running errands, tying back her hair with blue and green scarves. And when the children grow, she teaches them the steps of the dance, extending the tradition and instilling a love of movement. Today, Yia-Yia dances at the church festivals. When the sailor's song begins, everyone stops to watch as she "throws back her head" and "her dark, silver-streaked hair comes alive like a moonless night lit by shimmering silver stars."[2] The story highlights a memorable woman whose cultural traditions educate and inspire readers.

Anderson's second short story, "Passport," appeared in the young adult collection *Dirty Laundry* (1998), edited by Lisa Rowe Fraustino. As a result of his parents' divorce, Jared, a senior in high school, shuttles between the Land of Mom and the Kingdom of Dad, maintaining his role as a "six-foot-two Demilitarized Zone with bad skin."[3] Mom drops a steady collection of college applications in his lap, and Dad issues regular reminders to visit with Sergeant Payne and gear up for Army boot camp. Jared has his eyes on another option, however, and waits for his escape to arrive in the mail. He waits while his mother opens a custom-order curtain business in the house, covering the walls with false windows and chintz and gingham and corduroy. He waits while his dad begins a relationship with Heather, a young beauty just three years older than Jared. He waits while his mother deliberates over her revenge plan once she meets Heather, and he waits while his dad suffers the sadness of losing Heather to a golfing buddy who offers more than just jewelry and a fur coat. And then it arrives. His passport, the document that promises an end to his involvement in this war on the home front.

Reviewers loved the tale, calling it the "funniest story" in the collection.[4] In this "hilarious story of a boy who must reconcile his parents' post-high-school expectations of him with his own plans to travel,"[5] Anderson "takes an amusing look at a young person torn between divorced parents and struggling to create a reality all his own."[6]

Anderson's short story "Snake" appeared in Michael Cart's 2001 young adult collection *Love and Sex: Ten Stories of Truth*. It features two teens, one male and one female, whose inner thoughts are interspersed and intertwined amid the plot and dialogue. Adam, a California surfing teen, dreads having to entertain his father's boss's daughter while the two men conduct their business. Likewise, Lily, a gymnast and feminist from Buffalo, New York, is tired of being pawned off on different boys as her dad drags her along on his "seven-city tour of his nasty carpet showrooms."[7] The two end up at Venice Beach, where Lily is enthralled by the scene—"rollerbladers in bathing suits whiz by the artists, musicians, massage therapists, and sunglass salesmen lining the concrete boardwalk."[8] Lily drools over the chiseled men on Muscle Beach and proves her own strength by completing more pull-ups than her date can muster—which he finds pretty hot. When Lily's father calls to say he can't make dinner after all, Lily tosses the phone onto the sand, Adam tosses his uncomfortable shoes in the trash, and both strip off a layer of clothing and experience a sense of liberation. As they walk along the boardwalk, Lily is inexplicably drawn to a snake coiled around the arms of a woman and accepts the offer to hold it herself. When she does, "lightning crackles" under her skin.[9] Adam feels it, too, and the two share a moment of connection. Without a word, they head to the water, where their growing attraction proves indomitable and leads to a kiss.

At the conclusion of the story, Anderson explains her decision to set the tale in Venice, noting, "There is a freedom on the West Coast, an openness to explore identity and sexuality that is not found anywhere else. . . . For me, California is the Garden of Eden before God got pissed, a paradise of eternal adolescence."[10] Reviewer Patty Campbell agreed that "the setting of wacky, tacky Venice Beach" suits the tale just fine.[11]

POEMS

With respect to herself as a poet, Anderson says, "I do write poetry, but it is private. Well, so far it's been private. Poetry is the form I turn to when I am depressed or afraid."[12] As a result of her desire to keep this form of writing to herself, Anderson has not yet formally published any poems. However, she has made some pieces public through her live journal and through promotional materials released as part of the tenth anniversary celebration of *Speak*.

In various posts on her live journal, Anderson expresses her feelings through haiku, the poetry form her second grade teacher taught her to love. Many of these pieces reflect Anderson's frustrations tinged with humor. In response to her broken computer, for example, she writes:

> The bubonic plague
> infecting with tendrils gray
> Powerbook weeping.[13]

Similarly, when she suffers a painfully slow Amtrak ride, she concludes:

> Hours late again
> We tried to submit, accept
> Train zen is a crock.[14]

Another piece offers more celebration than complaint, an ode to food as fuel:

Sublime breakfast food
Oatmeal Raisin Powerbar
Carbo-hydrate me.[15]

A few of these online poems stray from the haiku and take on a more free verse form. Anderson comments on an autumn day when she writes:

Gary and Jim sell me thin-skinned apples
—trees bristling like greedy porcupines—melancholy, sour-sweet apples.
Winter stalks.[16]

And she commends the dedicated teachers who flock each year to the annual workshop of the Assembly on Literature for Adolescents (ALAN) with these words:

ALAN: adore,
applaud loud the
crowd of teachers unbowed,
proud to defy the lowering clouds
that darken the horizon.

ALAN, a peal
of pure song singing silver
and gold foretold by storytellers
old, old to rekindle the hope of
children on the edge.[17]

Anderson's most widely known and emotionally revealing poem is "Listen." It was printed and posted as part of the events surrounding the tenth anniversary of the publication of Anderson's first novel, *Speak*. The first and last stanzas are Anderson's, while each line in between is crafted from words written by readers and sent to Anderson in letters or e-mail messages. The poem, in its entirety, reads:

You write to us
from Houston, Brooklyn, Peoria, Rye, NY,
LA, DC, Everyanywhere USA to my mailbox, My
Space Face

Book
A livejournal of bffs whispering
Onehundredthousand whispers to Melinda and
Me.

You:
I was raped, too
sexually assaulted in seventh grade,
tenth grade, the summer after graduation,
at a party
i was 16
i was 14
i was 5 and he did it for three years
i loved him
i didn't even know him.
He was my best friend's brother,
my grandfather, father, mommy's boyfriend,
my date
my cousin
my coach
i met him for the first time that night and—
four guys took turns, and—
i'm a boy and this happened to me, and—
. . . I got pregnant I gave up my daughter for adoption . . .
did it happen to you, too?
U 2?

You:
i wasn't raped, but
my dad drinks, but
i hate talking, but
my brother was shot, but
i am outcast, but
my parents split up, but
i am clanless, but
we lost our house, but
i have secrets—seven years of secrets
and i cut
myself my friends cut
we all cut cut cut
to let out the pain

. . . my 5-year-old cousin was raped—
he's beginning to act out now . . .
do you have suicidal thoughts?
do you want to kill him?

You:
Melinda is a lot like this girl I know
No she's a lot like
(me)
i am MelindaSarah
i am MelindaRogelio i am MelindaMegan,
MelindaAmberMelindaStephenTori
PhillipNavdiaTiaraMateoKristinaBeth
it keeps hurting, but
but
but
but
this book cracked my shell
it keeps hurting I hurt, but
but your book cracked my shell.

You:
I cried when I read it.
I laughed when I read it
is that dumb?
I sat with the girl—
you know, that girl—
I sat with her because nobody sits with her at lunch
and I'm a cheerleader, so there.

speak changed my life
cracked my shell
made me think
about parties
gave me
wings this book
opened my mouth
i whispered, cried
rolled up my sleeves i
hate talking but
I am trying.

You made me remember who I am.
Thanks.

P.S. Our class is gonna analyze this thing to death.

Me:
Me:
Me: weeping.[18]

Anderson has taken raw emotion, earnest and honest words of pain and admission, and crafted them into a piece that sears the memory and creates a difficult but necessary sense of interconnectedness. Given the power of this piece, Anderson, the poet, has much to offer. Yet she insists that, with the exception of "Listen," poetry will remain "a private experience."

Anderson's shorter pieces contain many elements inherent in Anderson's longer works. In her short stories, Anderson creates characters that are believable and richly drawn. As they face realistic (and often universal) obstacles, they learn and grow over the arc of the narrative. In her poems, Anderson uses language with intention and care. Sometimes lyrical, sometimes humorous, her words convey meaning and inspire emotional responses. In both her short stories and poems, Anderson demands much of her readers by asking them to consider their assumptions of self and others. In these shorter works, however, Anderson does so with increased efficiency, using characters and language to affect readers in just a few, memorable pages.

NOTES

1. Laurie Halse Anderson, "Yia-Yia's Dance," *Highlights for Children*, 1 January 1998, www.HighlightsKids.com.
2. Anderson, "Yia-Yia's Dance."
3. Laurie Halse Anderson, "Passport," in *Dirty Laundry*, ed. Lisa Rowe Fraustino (New York: Viking, 1998), 128.
4. Hazel Rochman, *Booklist*, 15 May 1998.
5. *Kirkus Reviews*, 1 May 1998.
6. Brangien Davis, *Amazon.com* Review, www.amazon.com.
7. Laurie Halse Anderson, "Snake," in *Love and Sex: Ten Stories of Truth*, ed. Michael Cart (New York: Simon and Schuster, 2001), 90.

8. Anderson, "Snake," 96.

9. Anderson, "Snake," 103.

10. Anderson, "Snake," 106.

11. Patty Campbell, *Amazon.com* Review, www.amazon.com.

12. Laurie Halse Anderson, "Live Journal," 8 February 2006, http://halseanderson.livejournal.com.

13. Laurie Halse Anderson, "Live Journal," 20 April 2006, http://halseanderson.livejournal.com.

14. Laurie Halse Anderson, "Live Journal," 14 June 2006, http://halseanderson.livejournal.com.

15. Laurie Halse Anderson, "Live Journal," 28 March 2007, http://halseanderson.livejournal.com.

16. Laurie Halse Anderson, "Live Journal," 13 September 2006, http://halseanderson.livejournal.com.

17. Laurie Halse Anderson, "Live Journal," 19 November 2007, http://halseanderson.livejournal.com.

18. Laurie Halse Anderson, "Listen," *Speak Discussion Guide*, Puffin Books Marketing, 2008, http://speakupaboutspeak.blogspot.com.

Chapter Twelve

━━━━━━━━━━━━━━━━━━━━◯━━━━━━━━━━━━━━━━━━━━

A Life of Passion

IN ADDITION TO WRITING stories that encourage readers to reconsider and potentially reconstruct their personal identities and think about their place in the larger social community, Laurie Halse Anderson lives as she writes. She embraces the difficult questions and strives to live harmoniously with others and her world, even in the face of opposition or difficulty. Her passion—for young people, young adult literature, the local and global community, and graceful living—unites her identities as a storyteller and a person.

PASSION FOR KIDS

Anderson genuinely cares about the young people for whom she writes. She refuses to talk down to, patronize, or belittle teens and the concerns they express—or that they keep hidden away. She is their advocate, valuing their realities and defending their perspectives, all while helping them develop a more complex understanding of their rights and responsibilities as adolescents soon to be adults. Her story ideas grow from their messages and letters, and her online posts reveal a regular commitment to soliciting their insights. In response to a discussion surrounding the use of profanity in young adult novels, for example, she asks her readers to share their opinions. She queries, "What do you think? Should characters in books for teenagers (grades 9–12) use curse words? Is it realistic? Is it realistic to have a book for teenagers in which the characters don't curse?"[1]

In providing this forum, she demonstrates her trust in young people to discuss potentially contentious issues and share and develop their own understandings.

She expresses concern, too, that young people are losing the opportunity to work out personal understandings of literature. With the advent of new technologies, readers can locate the "correct" interpretation through a simple search and ask authors through online forums to explain "what they meant" when they wrote a given text. Anderson laments, "The notion of a student's personal interpretation of text is quickly vanishing. I hear from kids who want to know why I put a scene in, or what a symbol stands for. . . . While I have opinions about all of these things, I think the reader's interpretation is every bit (if not more!) valid than mine. That's why we read books—they can hold up a mirror that allows us to see ourselves more clearly. This is especially important when you are a teenager and half the time you have no clue who you are."[2]

Anderson remains hopeful, however, finding solace in and appreciation for young readers and their candor. She tells a story of a reader named Sam who writes, "I just read *Speak*, and it may be the best possible book I've ever read. I'm only in 7th grade but I read alot and your book is one of the best, of course after Stephen King." In response, Anderson says, "Of course, Sam. I totally understand."[3] And she totally does.

PASSION FOR THE FIELD

In support of the teen readers she so respects, Anderson adamantly defends the literature written for them, arguing repeatedly for its value and literary merit. In a live journal post dated 22 July 2008, she takes up arms against critics of young adult literature who argue that authors for teens don't deserve the same respect as authors of "real" literature.[4] She rants, "They don't respect us for writing YA? Who gives a damn what they think? People who don't understand the significance of YA literature to our culture are either ignorant or they are idiots." She ignores those who are ignorant, noting that they missed the revolution and that their opinions subsequently don't really matter, as they aren't grounded in any knowledge or understanding.

The idiots, however, remain subject to her wrath. She defines the idiots as those who "make grand pronouncements on literature, who believe that the best way to educate a 14-year-old who reads below grade level is to shove *Great Expectations* down his throat. Then, when the kid says that the book sucks and that all books suck, and he reaches for his game controller, they are shocked and appalled at this horrifying, illiterate generation." Idiots, she says, also come in the form of authors who "write dense short stories in which nothing happens that cause a sub-section of erudite inhabitants of Brooklyn to twitter and fawn, but leave the rest of the reading world scratching their heads." She struggles with how to address the critiques of those who define literature with a capital L, those who fail to recognize that everyone needs a good story, even those with less refined tastes. She considers her options: "I guess instead of flipping them the bird, I should try and be a little more understanding. . . . Or maybe not."

Anderson has also come forth in defense of YA titles in the debate involving the curriculum and the classics. While Anderson says she would love for all students to graduate with an understanding of and appreciation for the classics, she recognizes the more complex reality of students as readers in schools. The better (and more necessary) goal, she argues, should be for young people to leave school knowing how to read.[5] Given the publication dates and intended adult audience of classic titles, students who resist reading aren't likely to find much to change their impressions of the task. Instead, claims Anderson, "they find themselves fighting through dense text trying to understand situations and worlds that they have little or no connection to." Anderson bemoans the decline in reading interest she has witnessed among kids as they make the transition from elementary to secondary school. In the earlier grades, she argues, "we do a terrific job in America sparking the enthusiasm of kids for books—fiction and non-fiction. We hand them books that are appropriate for their age and reading level, and that have stories that connect to them." When students move to middle and high school, however, "many of them start hating books, largely because the books have no meaning for them, or are beyond their ability." Anderson is more than a writer; she's an advocate for classroom reform.

PASSION FOR THE COMMUNITY

Anderson does more than talk about change; she fosters it through her commitment to social justice and her generous spirit. In a live journal entry posted on 3 July 2005, she describes a concert held in Philadelphia designed to raise awareness around issues of poverty in Africa.[6] While Anderson commends the organizers and attendees, she encourages readers to dig a bit deeper and view the event through a more critical lens. She points out that the concert lasted for one day and that participants came out not to protest but to dance. While some emerged more educated, she makes it clear that there are real limits to the power and significance of such an event.

Anderson encourages readers to consider ways in which their efforts might achieve something more, might result in real social change, not simply awareness. She asks them to consider political involvement, from electing local and national leaders willing to put poverty on the agenda, to contacting a congressional representative about issues of concern, to volunteering on local party committees. She asks the harder question, "To those of you at the concert yesterday—were there any voter registration booths?" She also asks readers to consider issues of local poverty and determine ways in which they can make a difference in their own communities. She reminds them, "There are schools within a two-mile radius of yesterday's concert that do not have school libraries, because there is no budget for them. There are children who live in walking distance of yesterday's concert who went to bed hungry last night, who didn't have cable TV or the Internet to watch the concert, who have little hope, and few ways out. Poverty is everywhere." Anderson subtly reminds readers of their own privilege, planting a seed that might lead to an altered awareness and, ideally, action. And she nudges along this growth in a final jab:

> The irony of privileged Americans who drove fourteen hours in their gas-guzzling SUVs to Philadelphia, where they stayed in air-conditioned hotels so they could attend a free concert where they ate junk food to their heart's content and left trash barrels overflowing with unfinished hot dogs and funnel cakes in an effort to "Make Poverty History" is rather obvious. Doing something charitable because it makes you feel good is a start. Doing something charitable that will actually make the world a better place is even better. I urge you to action.

Anderson has engaged in such action through her generous donation of books to support multiple causes. After *Speak* was nominated for the National Book Award, Anderson hosted a party to celebrate. She asked each guest to bring a children's book to be donated to Philadelphia public school libraries in need. As a result of this effort, ninety-two books and $200 in cash were given to the McClure Elementary School, and Anderson also donated 180 autographed copies of *Ndito Runs*, one for every elementary school in the city.[7] Additionally, as part of a program to raise animal awareness among children—and increase access to books among young readers in financial need, Anderson donated forty sets of several titles in her *Vet Volunteers* series to children participating in a program sponsored by the Mexico, New York, Recreation Department and the Mexico Public Library.[8] Over the duration of the project, kids met each month and received copies of the next title in the series. To supplement their interest and understanding, they were visited by speakers from a zoo, a wildlife rehabilitation center, and at the final group meeting, Anderson herself.

PASSION FOR GRACEFUL LIVING

Anderson does what she can to enjoy life in the moment, to remind herself of her connection to something greater, to breathe and to laugh even when it seems most difficult to do so. She tells the story of being stuck in an airport after a cancelled flight and feeling the need to calm herself down.[9] She performed what she called the Airport Tea Ceremony and instructs readers on how to create such moments of Zen for themselves. First, one must purchase tea. While standing in line, Anderson encourages readers to "observe how the vicious ones belittle and demean the young woman who is earning minimum wage serving jerks coffee and doughnuts. Contemplate how those jerks are accumulating massive bad karma points. Smile at them when they walk by you. (It confuses them.)" She also advises readers to smile at the girl when placing the order, to talk to her and ask how her day is going. "Take your time," she intones. "Life is too fast and we need to savor these encounters. If you're lucky, she'll offer you some honey from the staff's secret stash." After adding milk to the tea, Anderson reminds readers to wait for a moment and watch how the colors swirl. As readers carry their tea to the gate, Anderson assures them that they won't find a seat and that's okay. "That's why you wear jeans to the airport." Sit on the floor, she instructs. "Don't worry about any critters or germs that live on the floor. We are all living beings." Sit, listen to music, smile, breathe. "Sip the tea. Taste the honey. Life is good."

THE PASSIONATE LIFE OF A TELLER OF TALES

The union of Anderson's passions as a writer and a person are embodied perfectly in the tattoo she wears, the Old English word Hwæt, on the inside of her right wrist. It is the first word in *Beowulf*, the oldest existing piece of Anglo-Saxon poetry, first told around the year 600 and written down around the year 1000. As Anderson explains, "Hwaet is the bard calling to the audience to listen to him/her. The storyteller, with this word, is basically saying 'Yo. Have a seat. Lend me your ears.'"[10] For Anderson, this sentiment represents "everything," her passions, her identities, her gift. "It connects me to the roots of my language and to my calling as a storyteller."[11]

Laurie Halse Anderson is the bard. Pull up a chair. Listen. Accept the story with grace. Let it change you.

NOTES

1. Laurie Halse Anderson, "Live Journal," 15 February 2005, http://halseanderson .livejournal.com.

2. Laurie Halse Anderson, "Live Journal," 4 March 2005, http://halseanderson .livejournal.com.

3. Laurie Halse Anderson, "Live Journal," 11 February 2005, http://halseanderson .livejournal.com.

4. Laurie Halse Anderson, "Live Journal," 22 July 2008, http://halseanderson .livejournal.com.

5. Laurie Halse Anderson, "Live Journal," 27 July 2006, http://halseanderson .livejournal.com.

6. Laurie Halse Anderson, "Live Journal," 3 July 2005, http://halseanderson .livejournal.com.

7. "Author Turns Loss into Gain," *School Library Journal* (March 2000): 109.

8. "Mexico Program to Aid Animals Gets Under Way," *Syracuse Post-Standard*, 17 September 2008.

9. Laurie Halse Anderson, "Live Journal," 31 March 2005, http://halseanderson .livejournal.com.

10. Laurie Halse Anderson, "Live Journal," 6 March 2007, http://halseanderson .livejournal.com.

11. Anderson, "Live Journal," 6 March 2007.

Appendix:
Honors and Awards

PERSONAL HONORS

Margaret A. Edwards Award, Young Adult Library Services Association, American Library Association, 2009

ALAN Award, Assembly on Literature for Adolescents, National Council of Teachers of English, 2008

Onondaga Community College Alumni Faces Award, 2006

Fayetteville-Manlius Hall of Distinction, 2004

Free Library of Philadelphia/Drexel University Children's Literature Citation, 2002

LITERARY AWARDS

Catalyst

Best Books for Young Adults, Young Adult Library Services Association, American Library Association, 2003

Best Teen Book, Barnes & Noble, 2002

Books for the Teen Age, New York Public Library, 2003

Borders Original Voices Finalist, 2002

Evergreen Young Adult Book Award Nominee (Washington), 2005

Garden State Teen Book Award Nominee (New Jersey), 2005

Gateway Readers Award Nominee (Missouri Association School Librarians), 2004–2005

Iowa High School Book Award Nominee, 2004–2005
Kentucky Bluegrass Award Nominee, 2003
Pennsylvania School Librarians Association YA Top Forty, 2003
Rhode Island Teen Book Award Nominee, 2003
Tayshas High School Reading List (Texas), 2004–2005
Thumbs Up! Award Nominee (Michigan), 2003
Top Ten Best Books for Young Adults, Young Adult Library Services Association, American Library Association, 2003
Top Ten Bestsellers, BookSense, Winter 2002–2003
Virginia Young Readers High School Nominee, 2002–2003
Washington State Award for Young Adult Books Winner, 2004
Young Readers Choice Award Nominee (Pacific Northwest Library Association), 2005

Chains

Best Book, *Publisher's Weekly*, 2008
Best Books for Young Adults, Young Adult Library Services Association, American Library Association, 2009
National Book Award Finalist in Young People's Literature, 2009
Notable Book, Association for Library Service to Children, American Library Association, 2009
Pennsylvania Young Readers Choice, Young Adult List, 2009–2010
Scott O'Dell Award Winner, 2009
Top Ten Best Books for Teens, Amazon.com, 2008

Fever 1793

100 Best Books of Fall, New York Public Library, 2000
100 Best of the Best for the 21st Century, Young Adult Library Association, American Library Association, 1994–2003, 2005
Beehive Award Nominee (Utah), 2003
Best Books for Young Adults, Young Adult Library Services Association, American Library Association, 2001
Best Children's Book of the Year, Bank Street College of Education, 2001
Books for the Teen Age, New York Public Library, 2001, 2002, 2004, 2005, 2006

California Young Reader Medal Nominee, 2004
Children's Book-of-the-Month Club Selection, 2000
Free Library of Philadelphia/Drexel University Children's Literature Citation Recipient, 2002
Garden State Teen Book Award Nominee (New Jersey), 2003
Georgia Children's Book Award Nominee, 2002–2003
Golden Sower Young Adult Honor Book (Nebraska), 2003
Great Lakes Great Books Award Winner (Michigan), 2003
Iowa Teen Book Award Master List, 2003–2004
Jefferson Cup Honor Book, 2001
Junior Library Guild Selection, 2000
Kentucky Bluegrass Award Nominee, 2001
Mark Twain Award Runner-up (Missouri), 2003
Massachusetts Children's Book Award Honor Book, 2003
Maud Hart Lovelace Youth Reading Award Nominee (Minnesota), 2003
Nevada Young Readers' Award Nominee, 2003
Nutmeg Award Nominee (Connecticut), 2002, 2003
Parent's Guide to Children's Media Award Winner, 2000
Pick of the Lists, American Booksellers Association, 2000
Popular Paperbacks for Young Adults, Young Adult Library Services Association, American Library Association, 2006
Rebecca Caudill Young Readers' Master List (Illinois), 2003
South Carolina Young Adult Book Award Nominee, 2002–2003
Sunshine State Reader Nominee (Florida), 2004–2005
Tayshas High School Reading List (Texas), 2001–2002
Teacher's Choice, International Reading Association, 2001
Virginia Young Reader's Award Nominee, 2003
Volunteer State Book Award Runner-up (Tennessee), 2002–2003
Young Hoosier Book Award Nominee (Indiana)

Fight for Life

Henry Bergh ASPCA Award for Children's Books, 2000

Ndito Runs

Pick of the Lists Multicultural Title, American Booksellers Association, 1996

Prom

Abraham Lincoln Illinois High School Book Award Semifinalist, 2006
Books for the Teen Age, New York Public Library, 2006
Capitol Choice Award Nominee (District of Columbia), 2006
Junior Library Guild Selection, 2005
Kentucky Bluegrass Award Nominee, 2006
New York Times Bestseller
Oregon Young Adult Network Book Rave, 2007
Quick Picks for Young Adults, Young Adult Library Services Association,
    American Library Association, 2006
South Carolina Young Adult Book Award Nominee, 2007–2008
Tayshas High School Reading List (Texas), 2006–2007
Top Shelf Fiction for Middle School Readers, Voice of Youth Advocates,
    2005
Top Ten Best Books for Teens, Amazon.com, 2005
Top Ten Bestseller List, *BookSense*, Spring 2005
Volunteer State Young Adult Book Award Winner (Tennessee), 2006
Young Adults' Choice, International Reading Association, 2007

Say Good-bye

Children's Book Council Children's Choice, 2002

Speak

100 Best of the Best for the 21st Century, Young Adult Library Services
    Association, American Library Association, 1994–2003, 2005
Abraham Lincoln Illinois High School Book Award Runner-up, 2001
Best Books for Young Adults, Young Adult Library Services Association,
    American Library Association, 2000
Best Books of the Year, *Publishers Weekly*, 1999
Best Books of the Year, *School Library Journal*, 1999
Black-Eyed Susan Book Award Winner (Maryland), 2002–2003
Books for the Teen Age, New York Public Library, 2000, 2001
Bulletin of the Center for Children's Books Blue Ribbon Book, 1999
California Young Reader Medal Nominee, 2002–2003

Carolyn W. Field Award (Pennsylvania), 2000
Edgar Allan Poe Award Finalist, 2000
Editors' Choice, *Booklist*, 2000
Evergreen Young Adult Book Award Winner (Washington), 2002
Fanfare Honor Book, *Horn Book*, 1999
Garden State Teen Book Award Winner (New Jersey), 2002
Golden Kite Award for Fiction Winner, Society of Children's Book Writers and Illustrators, 1999
Heartland Award Winner (Kansas), 2001
Iowa Teen Book Award Nominee, 2001–2002
Junior Library Guild Selection, 1999
Kentucky Bluegrass Award Winner, 2001
Los Angeles Times Book Prize Finalist, 2000
Maud Hart Lovelace Youth Reading Award Nominee (Minnesota), 2005
Michael L. Printz Honor Book, Young Adult Library Services Association, American Library Association, 2000
National Book Award Finalist in Young People's Literature, 1999
Nevada Young Readers' Award Nominee, 2003
New York Reads Together Book, 2005
New York Times Bestseller
Pennsylvania Young Readers Choice Young Adult List, 2001–2002
Popular Paperbacks for Young Adults, Young Adult Library Services Association, American Library Association, 2003
Quick Picks for Young Adults, Young Adult Library Services Association, American Library Association, 2000
Rhode Island Teen Book Award Nominee, 2001
Sequoyah Book Award Winner (Oklahoma), 2002
South Carolina Young Adult Book Award Winner, 2001–2002
Tayshas High School Reading List (Texas), 2001–2002
Teen Three Apples Book Award Nominee (New York), 2009
Top Ten Best Books for Young Adults, Young Adult Library Services Association, American Library Association, 2000
Top Ten First Novels, *Booklist*, 1999
Volunteer State Young Adult Book Award Winner (Tennessee), 2002
Washington State Award for Young Adult Books, 2002
Young Adult Choice, International Reading Association, 2001

Thank You, Sarah

Amelia Bloomer List, Association of Library Services to Children, American Library Association, 2002
Black-Eyed Susan Award Nominee (Maryland), 2003–2004
Capitol Choices Book (Washington, D.C.), 2002
Carolyn W. Field Honor Book (Pennsylvania), 2003
Center for Children's Books Best Book, 2002
Chapman Award for Shared Reading Recipient, 2002
Garden State Book Award Nominee (New Jersey), 2005
Junior Library Guild Selection, 2002
North Carolina Children's Book Award Nominee, 2004
Notable Video, Young Adult Library Services Association, American Library Association, 2005
Once Upon a World Children's Book Award Winner, Simon Wiesenthal Center, 2003
Oppenheimer Toy Portfolio Gold Award Winner, 2003
PBS TeacherSource Recommended Social Studies Book: Civic and Community, 2005
Second Grade Selection, Governor's Book Club (New Jersey), 2003
Show Me Readers Award Nominee (Missouri), 2004–2005
South Carolina Children's Book Award Nominee, 2005–2006
Storytelling World Honor Title, 2004
Teacher's Choice Award Winner, International Reading Association, 2003
Young Hoosier Award Nominee (Indiana)

Trapped

Teacher's Choice, International Reading Association, 2009

Turkey Pox

Parent's Choice Honor Book, 1999
South Carolina Book Award Nominee

Twisted

Amazon Editor's Pick for Teens, 2007
Best Books for the Teen Age, New York Public Library, 2008
Best Books for Young Adults, Young Adult Library Services Association, American Library Association, 2008
Borders YA Book Club Pick, 2008
Eliot Rosewater Indiana High School Book Award Winner, Indiana Library Foundation, 2008–2009
Georgia Peach Book Award Nominee, 2008–2009
Heartland Award Nominee (Kansas), 2008
Kentucky Bluegrass Award Master List, 2009
New York Times Bestseller, 2008
Quick Picks for Young Adults, Young Adult Library Services Association, American Library Association, 2008
Sequoyah Book Award Masterlist (Oklahoma), 2010
Tayshas High School Reading List (Texas), 2008
Thumbs Up! Award Honor Book (Michigan), 2008
Top Ten of 2007, International Reading Association, 2008

Wintergirls

Editor's Choice, *New York Times*
Kentucky Bluegrass Award Master List, 2010

Bibliography

PRIMARY WORKS

Picture Books

The Big Cheese of Third Street. New York: Simon and Schuster, 2002.
The Hair of Zoe Fleefenbacher Goes to School. New York: Simon and Schuster, 2009.
Independent Dames: What You Never Knew about the Women and Girls of the American Revolution. New York: Simon and Schuster, 2008.
Ndito Runs. New York: Henry Holt, 1996.
No Time for Mother's Day. Morton Grove, Ill.: Albert Whitman, 1999.
Saudi Arabia (A Ticket to). Minneapolis, Minn.: Carolrhoda Books, 2001.
Thank You, Sarah: The Woman Who Saved Thanksgiving. New York: Simon and Schuster, 2002.
Turkey Pox. Morton Grove, Ill.: Albert Whitman, 1996.

Chapter Books

End of the Race. Middleton, Wis.: Pleasant Company, 2002; Puffin, 2005.
Fear of Falling. Middleton, Wis.: Pleasant Company, 2001; Puffin, 2009.
Fight for Life. Middleton, Wis.: Pleasant Company, 2000; Puffin, 2007.
Homeless: Sunita. Middleton, Wis.: Pleasant Company, 2000; Puffin, 2007.
Manatee Blues. Middleton, Wis.: Pleasant Company, 2000; Puffin, 2008.

Masks. Middleton, Wis.: Pleasant Company, 2002; Puffin, 2005.
Say Goodbye. Middleton, Wis.: Pleasant Company, 2001; Puffin, 2008.
Storm Rescue. Middleton, Wis.: Pleasant Company, 2001; Puffin, 2008.
Teacher's Pet. Middleton, Wis.: Pleasant Company, 2001; Puffin, 2009.
Time to Fly. Middleton, Wis.: Pleasant Company, 2002; Puffin, 2009.
Trapped. Middleton, Wis.: Pleasant Company, 2001; Puffin, 2009.
The Trickster. Middleton, Wis.: Pleasant Company, 2000; Puffin, 2008.

Young Adult Novels

Catalyst. New York: Viking, 2002.
Chains. New York: Simon and Schuster, 2008.
Fever 1793. New York: Simon and Schuster, 2000.
Prom. New York: Viking, 2005.
Speak. New York: Farrar, Straus and Giroux, 1999.
Twisted. New York: Viking, 2007.
Wintergirls. New York: Viking, 2009.

Short Stories

"Passport." 128–39 in *Dirty Laundry*, edited by Lisa Rowe Fraustino. New York: Viking, 1998.
"Snake," 89–107 in *Love and Sex: Ten Stories of Truth*, edited by Michael Cart. New York: Simon and Schuster, 2001.
"Yia-Yia's Dance." *Highlights for Children*, 1 January 1998. www.Highlights Kids.com.

Poem

"Listen." *Speak Discussion Guide*. Puffin, 2008. http://speakupaboutspeak.blogspot.com.

Essays and Speeches

"Acceptance Speech for the Golden Kite Award in Fiction." Speech presented at the Annual SCBWI Summer Conference, Los Angeles, California, 30 July 2000. www.scbwi.org.

"Behind the Book." *Author Website*. www.writerlady.com/novelsh/ch_behind
.html.

"College Peasure Essay: What Your Guidance Counselor Didn't Tell You
. . . and Your Parents Don't Know." *Author Website*. www.writerlady.com/
novelsh/c_essay.html.

"Frequently Asked Questions." *Author Website*. www.writerlady.com/faqh
.html.

"Interview with the Author." *Speak*. New York: Penguin, 2009.

"Interview with the Author." *Speak*. New York: Puffin, 2001, 2006.

"Live Journal." http://halseanderson.livejournal.com.

"Loving the Young Adult Reader Even When You Want to Strangle Him
(or Her)!" *ALAN Review* 32, no. 2 (2005): 53–58.

"The Mystery and Magic of Story: A Spell That Connects One Heart to
Another." *ALAN Review* 34, no. 1 (2006): 5–7.

"Recycling Our Thinking." In *Recycle This Book: 100 Top Children's Book
Authors Tell You How to Go Green*, edited by Dan Gutman. New York:
Yearling, 2009.

The Shy Child: Helping Children Triumph over Shyness. (With Ward K.
Swallow.) New York: Grand Central, 2000.

"*Speak* Movie Pages." *Author Website*. www.writerlady.com/speakmovie
.html.

"Speaking Out." *ALAN Review* 27, no. 3 (2000): 25–26.

"Speaking Truth to Power." Speech delivered at the Annual Workshop of
the Assembly on Literature for Adolescents, San Antonio, Texas, 15
November 2008.

"Teachers' Guide for *Fever 1793*." *Author Website*. www.writerlady.com/
novelsh/f_guide.html.

"Up for Discussion—The Writing of *Fever 1793*: A Historical Detective
Searches for the Truth." *School Library Journal*, 1 May 2001.

SECONDARY WORKS

"2008 National Book Award Finalist, Young People's Literature." *National
Book Foundation Interview*, 2008. www.nationalbook.org/nba2008_ypl_
anderson.html.

"2009 Youth Media Awards Winner Calls." *American Libraries Association*, 11 February 2009. http://alfocus.ala.org/videos/2009-youth-media-awards-winner-calls.

Alsup, Janet. "Politicizing Young Adult Literature: Reading Anderson's *Speak* as a Critical Text." *Journal of Adolescent and Adult Literacy* 47, no. 2 (2003): 158–66.

Ames, Melissa. "Memoirs of a Bathroom Stall: The Women's Lavatory as Crying Room, Confessional, and Sanctuary." *EAPSU Online: A Journal of Critical and Creative Work* 3 (Fall 2006): 63–74.

Anderson, Stephanie Holcomb. "About Me." *Author Website*, 2004. www.writerlady.com/me.html.

———. "Officially Long Official Biography of Laurie Halse Anderson." *Author Website*, 2008. www.writerlady.com/bioh.html.

Atkins, Holly. "An Interview with Laurie Halse Anderson." *St. Petersburg Times: Tampa Bay*, 15 December 2003. www.sptimes.com.

"Author Turns Loss into Gain." *School Library Journal* (March 2000): 109.

"Authors: Interviews: Laurie Halse Anderson." *YA and Kids Books Central*, August 2005. http://yabookscentral.com.

"Authors Unleashed: Interview with Laurie Halse Anderson." *TeensRead-Too*, 24 January 2009. http://authorsunleashed.blogspot.com.

Blasingame, James. "Interview with Laurie Halse Anderson." *Journal of Adolescent and Adult Literacy* 49, no. 1 (September 2005): 72–73.

"Books into Movies." *Teenreads.com*. www.teenreads.com/features/books2movies.asp.

Bott, C. J. "Why We Must Read Young Adult Books That Deal with Sexual Content." *ALAN Review* 34, no. 3 (2006): 26–29.

Boyd, Elizabeth Meckley. "Lost and Found: Female Voice in Laurie Halse Anderson's *Speak* and Nikki Grimes' *Bronx Masquerade*." Unpublished master's thesis, University of North Carolina, Charlotte, 2006.

Brown, Jennifer M. "In Dreams Begin Possibilities." 24–25 in "Flying Starts: Six Authors and Illustrators with Well-Received Fall Debuts Talk about Their Work." *Publisher's Weekly*, 20 December 1999.

Buehler, Jennifer. "A Conversation with Laurie Halse Anderson." *Read. Write.Think Podcasts and Videos*, 28 February 2009. www.readwrite think.org/beyondtheclassroom/summer/podcastsvideos/TextMessages/12LaurieHalseAnderson_detail.asp.

Calhoun, Dia, and Lorie Ann Grover. "rgz tv: Laurie Halse Anderson, 2009." *Readergirlz*, 25 March 2009. http://readergirlz.blogspot.com/2009/03/rgz-tv-laurie-halse-anderson-2009_8255.html.

Castellitto, Linda M. "Making History Come Alive for Young Readers." *First Person Book Page*, November 2008. www.bookpage.com.

Corbett, Sue. "A Talk with Five NBA Finalists (or: What I Saw Underneath the Disreputable Chains of the Spectacular Now)." *Publisher's Weekly*, 30 October 2008.

Criswell, Mandy. "Laurie Halse Anderson." *Pennsylvania Center for the Book.* http://pabook.libraries.psu.edu.

Crook, John. "*Speak* Loud Enough for Showtime/Lifetime." *National Society of Film Critics*, 3 September 2005. http://tv.zap2it.com/tveditorial.

Dimmitt, Jean Pollard. "The First Printz Award Designations: Winners All." *ALAN Review* 28, no. 2 (2001).

Dowty, Douglass. "Mexico Author Finishes a Runner-up for National Book Awards." *Post-Standard*, 19 November 2008. www.syracuse.com.

"Dying on the Inside." *Memphis Parent*, 1 February 2009. www.memphisparent.com/2009/02/dying-on-the-inside.

"Dying to Be Thin." *National Public Radio.* 20 March 2009. www.hereandnow.org.

"Exclusive Q&A with Laurie Halse Anderson." *Teen Books (and Beyond!).* Palatine, Ill: Palatine Public Library, 17 February 2009. http://palatinelibraryteens.blogspot.com.

Fineman, Kelly R. "Laurie Halse Anderson." *Writing and Ruminating: One Children's Writer's Journey*, 19 May 2008. http://kellyrfineman.livejournal.com.

Fitzgerald, Carol, and Marisa Emralino. "Interview with Laurie Halse Anderson." *Teenreads.com* (August 2005). www.teenreads.com/authors.

Florence, Debbi Michiko. "An Interview with Children's Author Laurie Halse Anderson." www.debbimichikoflorence.com.

Franzak, Judith, and Elizabeth Noll. "Monstrous Acts: Problematizing Violence in Young Adult Literature." *Journal of Adolescent and Adult Literacy* 49, no. 8 (2006): 662–72.

Gallo, Don. "Laurie Halse Anderson." *Authors4Teens.* www.authors4teens.com/introduction.jsp?authorid=landerson.

Goodnow, Cecelia. "Laurie Halse Anderson: It Ain't Easy Being Teen." *Seattle Post-Intelligencer*, 17 March 2009.

Haugsted, Linda. "Showtime, Lifetime *Speak* Together." *Multichannel News*, 23 July 2005.

Hedblad, Alan, ed. "Laurie Halse Anderson." 1–3 in *Something about the Author*, vol. 95. Detroit, Mich.: Gale Research, 1998.

Hicks, Betty. "Meet Laurie Halse Anderson." *Children's Literature*, 2000. www.childrenslit.com/childrenslit/mai_anderson_laurie.html.

Hill, Christine M. "Laurie Halse Anderson Speaks: An Interview." *Voice of Youth Advocates* 23, no. 5 (2000): 325–27.

Hipple, Ted, and Jennifer L. Claiborne. "The Best Young Adult Novels of All Time, or *The Chocolate War* One More Time." *English Journal* 94, no. 3 (2005): 99–102.

Horning, Kathleen T. "Fearless: An Interview with Laurie Halse Anderson." *School Library Journal*, 1 June 2009. www.schoollibraryjournal.com/article/CA6660876.html.

Jackett, Mark. "Something to *Speak* About: Addressing Sensitive Issues through Literature." *English Journal* 96, no. 4 (2007): 102–5.

Just, Julie. "Interview with Laurie Halse Anderson." *Inside the New York Times Book Review*, 2009. http://graphics8.nytimes.com/podcasts/2009/05/08/08bookreview.mp3.

Kaywell, Joan F., and Stephen Kaywell. "A Conversation with Laurie Halse Anderson." *Journal of Adolescent and Adult Literacy* 52, no. 1 (2008): 78–83.

Larson, Kirby. "Laurie Halse Anderson Speaks." 23 March 2009. http://kirbyslane.blogspot.com/2009/03/laurie-halse-anderson-speaks.html.

Latham, Don. "Melinda's Closet: Trauma and the Queer Subtext of Laurie Halse Anderson's *Speak*." *Children's Literature Association Quarterly* 31, no. 4 (2006): 369–82.

"Laurie Halse Anderson." *Authors and Artists for Young Adults*, vol. 39. Farmington Hills, Mich.: Gale Group, 2001. Reproduced in Biography Resource Center. Farmington Hills, Mich.: Thomson Gale, 2007.

"Laurie Halse Anderson." *Simon and Schuster Website*. http://authors.simonandschuster.com/Laurie-Halse-Anderson.

"Laurie Halse Anderson 2009 on *Chains*." *Bookfiends Kingdom*. www.bfkbooks.com/node/791.

"Laurie Halse Anderson Chats with Readergirlz." *Readergirlz*. 23 June 2008. www.mitaliblog.com/search/label/Author%20Interviews.

"Laurie Halse Anderson Discusses *Wintergirls*." *Speak Up about Speak*, 1 April 2009. www.speakupaboutspeak.blogspot.com.

Lesesne, Teri S., and Rosemary Chance. "Speak." 47–48 in *Hit List for Young Adults 2: Frequently Challenged Books*. Chicago: American Library Association, 2002.

"Let's Welcome Laurie Halse Anderson to The Family Room!" *Barnes and Noble Online Bookclub*, 30 June–4 July 2008. http://bookclubs.barnesand noble.com/bn/board.

Little Willow. "Interview: Laurie Halse Anderson." *Slayground*. 5 August 2007. http://slayground.livejournal.com.

Mack, Diane. "*Chains* Sees the Revolutionary War through the Eyes of the Young." *National Public Radio*. 13 November 2008. www.publicbroad casting.net.

"Margaret A. Edwards Award: 2009 Winner." *American Library Association*. www.ala.org/ala/mgrps/divs/yalsa.

McVoy, Terra Elan. "Laurie Halse Anderson Meet and Greet." *Terralan*, 22 April 2009. http://terraelan.com.

"Mexico Program to Aid Animals Gets Under Way." *Syracuse Post-Standard*, 17 September 2008.

Miller, sj. "'Speaking' the Walk, 'Speaking' the Talk: Embodying Critical Pedagogy to Teach Young Adult Literature." *English Education* 40, no. 2 (2008): 145–54.

Miskec, Jennifer, and Chris McGee. "My Scars Tell a Story: Self-Mutilation in Young Adult Literature." *Children's Literature Association Quarterly* 32, no. 2 (2007): 163–78.

Morales, Macey, and Jennifer Petersen. "Laurie Halse Anderson Wins 2009 Edwards Award for Significant and Lasting Contribution to Young Adult Readers for 'Catalyst,' 'Fever 1793,' and 'Speak.'" *American Library Association Press Release*, 26 January 2009. www.ala.org.

Newman, Patricia M. "Who Wrote That? Featuring Laurie Halse Anderson." *California Kids*, March 2005. www.patriciamnewman.com/anderson.html.

Ott, Bill. "A Century of Books: Children's and YA Authors Look Back." *Booklist*, 15 October 2004, 398.

Parker-Pope, Tara. "The Troubling Allure of Eating-Disorder Books." *New York Times Health*, 11 May 2009. http://well.blogs.nytimes.com.

Prince, Julie. "Writing from the Heart: An Interview with Laurie Halse Anderson." *Teacher Librarian* 36, no. 2 (2008): 70–71.

"Q and A Session." Kepler's Bookstore, Menlo Park, California, 10 April 2009. http://halseanderson.livejournal.com/.

"Q and A with Author Laurie Halse Anderson." *Penguin Group*, 2005. http://us.penguingroup.com.

"Q and A with Laurie Halse Anderson!" *YAthenaeum*, 6 January 2009. http://yathenaeum.blogspot.com.

Ressler, Diane, and Giannet, Stan. "Voices of Healing: How Creative Expression Therapies Help Us Heal, Using Laurie Halse Anderson's Novel, *Speak*, as a Springboard for Discussion." 185–205 in *Using Literature to Help Troubled Teenagers Cope with Abuse Issues*, edited by Joan F. Kaywell. Westport, Conn.: Greenwood, 2004.

Ryan, Laura T. "Central New York Author Nominated for National Book Award." *Post-Standard*, 16 October 2008. http://blog.syracuse.com/shelflife.

———. "Mexico Writer Plots Her Next Challenge: Half-marathon." *Post-Standard*, 10 June 2008. http://blog.syracuse.com/shelflife.

———. "More about *Wintergirls* and Laurie Halse Anderson." *Post-Standard*, 27 March 2009. http://blog.syracuse.com/shelflife.

———. "More from Laurie Halse Anderson." *Post-Standard*, 22 April 2007. http://blog.syracuse.com/shelflife.

Schwartz, Dana. "Interview with Laurie Halse Anderson." *Book Bag*. Available at *Teenreads.com*, August 2005. www.teenreads.com/authors.

"Showtime Independent Films Unspools *Speak* at AFI Fest on November 13th and 14th, 2004, at Arclight in Hollywood." *Market Wire*, November 2004. www.marketwire.com.

Speak (the film). *Fred Berner Films*, directed by Jessica Sharzer, 2005.

Spicer, Ed. "Interview with Laurie Halse Anderson." *Spicyreads*, 4 June 2008. www.spicyreads.com. See also Anderson, Laurie Halse. "Live Journal," 4 June 2008. http://halseanderson.livejournal.com.

Sprague, Marsha M., and Kara K. Keeling. "From *Fifteen* to *Speak*: Challenges Facing the Adolescent Girl in U.S. Society." 1–17 in *Discovering Their Voices: Engaging Adolescent Girls with Young Adult Literature*. Newark, Del.: International Reading Association, 2007.

Sprague, Marsha M., Kara K. Keeling, and Paul Lawrence. "'Today I'm going to meet a boy': Teachers and Students Respond to *Fifteen* and *Speak*." *ALAN Review* 34, no. 1 (2006): 25–32.

Tighe, Mary Ann. "Reviving Ophelia with Young Adult Literature." *ALAN Review* 33, no. 1 (2005): 56–61.

Verderame, Carla L. "Out of Silence into Speech: Two Perspectives of Growing Up Female." *ALAN Review* 28, no. 1 (2000).

"A Video Interview with Laurie Halse Anderson." *Adolescent Literacy*, 2009. www.adlit.org/transcript_display/28150.

Warner, Mary L. *Adolescents in the Search for Meaning: Tapping the Powerful Resource of Story*. Lanham, Md.: Scarecrow, 2006.

Wilde, Susan. "Talking with Laurie Halse Anderson." *Audiofile Magazine*, April/May 2009. www.audiofilemagazine.com/features/A2370.html.

Williams-Garcia, Rita. "Interview with Laurie Halse Anderson." *National Book Foundation*, 2008. www.nationalbook.org/nba2008_ypl_anderson _interv.html.

REVIEWS

The Big Cheese of Third Street

Cooper, Ilene. *Booklist*, 1 December 2001, 644.

Gallagher, Genevieve. *School Library Journal* (February 2002): 96.

Kirkus Reviews, 15 January 2002, 100.

Roback, Diane, Jennifer M. Brown, Jason Britton, and Jeff Zaleski. *Publishers Weekly*, 19 November 2001, 67.

Catalyst

Adams, Lauren. *Horn Book Magazine* 78, no. 6 (2002): 746.

Bryant, Lynn. *School Library Journal* (October 2002): 154.

Cooper, Ilene. *Booklist*, 15 September 2002, 222.

Hubert, Jennifer. *Amazon.com* Review. www.amazon.com.

Kirkus Reviews, 1 September 2002, 1300.

O'Hara, Roberta. *Teenreads.com*. www.teenreads.com/reviews.

Roback, Diane, Jennifer M. Brown, Jason Britton, and Jeff Zaleski. *Publishers Weekly*, 22 July 2002, 180.

Rohrlick, Paula. *Kliatt*, 1 September 2002.

Chains

Auger, Tanya D. *Horn Book* 84, no. 6 (2008): 696.

Bird, Elizabeth. *School Library Journal*, 4 October 2008.

Bush, Elizabeth. *Bulletin of the Center for Children's Books* 62, no. 3 (2008).
Christian Century, 16 December 2008.
Engberg, Gillian. *Booklist*, 1 November 2008, 42–43.
Faust, Susan. "Holiday Books: Young Readers." *San Francisco Gate*, 23 November 2008.
Fisher, Enicia. *Christian Science Monitor*, 2 January 2009.
Just, Julie. *New York Times Book Review*, 21 December 2008, 13.
Kirkus Reviews, 1 September 2008, 938.
Moore, Denise. *School Library Journal* (October 2008): 138.
Piehl, Norah. *Teenreads.com.* www.teenreads.com/reviews.
Prince, Julie M. *Teensreadtoo.* www.teensreadtoo.com/ChainsAnderson.html.
Publisher's Weekly, 1 September 2008, 53.
Quattlebaum, Mary. *Washington Post*, 30 November 2008.
Rosser, Claire. *Kliatt*, 1 September 2008.
Russell, Mary Harris. *Chicago Tribune*, 25 October 2008.

Fever 1793

Bradburn, Frances. *Booklist*, 1 October 2000, 332.
Burkam, Anita L. *Horn Book Magazine* 76, no. 5 (2000): 562–63.
Campbell, Patty. *Amazon.com* Review. www.amazon.com.
Isaacs, Kathleen. *School Library Journal* (August 2000): 177.
Karr, Kathleen. *Children's Literature*, 2000. http://childrenslit.com.
Kirkus Reviews, 15 June 2000.
Koorey, Stefani. *Voice of Youth Advocates.* (December 2000): 344.
New York Times Upfront, 13 November 2000.
Philadelphia Inquirer. 2000. www.writerlady.com/fever1793_reviews.html.
Publishers Weekly, 31 July 2000, 96.
Rohrlick, Paula. *Kliatt*, 1 March 2002.
Thompson, Constance Decker. *New York Times Book Review*, 19 November 2000, 45.
Zvirin, Stephanie. *Booklist* 98, no. 8, 15 December 2001, 728.

Fight for Life (Vet Volunteers #1)

Hicks, Betty. *Children's Literature*, 2000. http://childrenslit.com.
Peterson, Lauren. *Booklist*, 1 May 2000, 1665.

Praded, Joni. *Animals*, 1 November 2000.
Schomberg, Janie. *School Library Journal* (July 2000): 100.
Shaw, Martha. *Children's Literature*, 2000. http://childrenslit.com.

Homeless (Vet Volunteers #2)

Krasnow, Ronni. *School Library Journal* (December 2000): 138.
Tilly, Nancy. *Children's Literature*, 2000. http://childrenslit.com.

Independent Dames: What You Never Knew about the Women and Girls of the American Revolution

Auger, Tanya D. *Horn Book Magazine* 84, no. 5 (2008): 605.
Bock, Lee. *School Library Journal* (August 2008): 107–8.
Fineman, Kelly. "Writing and Ruminating," 17 May 2008. http://kellyr fineman.livejournal.com.
Gilson, Nancy. *Columbus Dispatch*, 2 July 2008.
Kirkus Reviews, 15 May 2008, 104.
McMahon, Regan. *San Francisco Gate*, 29 June 2008.
Publishers Weekly, 26 May 2008, 65–66.
School Library Journal (October 2008): 11.
Thereadingzone. http://thereadingzone.wordpress.com.

Ndito Runs

Devereaux, Elizabeth, and Diane Roback. *Publishers Weekly*, 18 March 1996, 68.
Hurlburt, Tom S. *School Library Journal* (May 1996): 84.
Rochman, Hazel. *Booklist*, 15 March 1996, 1268.

No Time for Mother's Day

Bulletin of the Center for Children's Books (April 1999): 271–72.
Burg, Roxanne. *School Library Journal* (April 1999): 85.
Cooper, Ilene. *Booklist*, 15 February 1999, 1073.
Jernigan, Gisela. *Children's Literature*, 2000. http://childrenslit.com.
Kirkus Reviews, 1 March 1999.

"Passport"

Davis, Brangien. *Amazon.com* Review. www.amazon.com.
Kirkus Reviews, 1 May 1998.
Rochman, Hazel. *Booklist*, 15 May 1998.

Prom

Adams, Lauren. *Horn Book Magazine* 81, no. 2 (2005): 196–97.
Blasingame, James. *Journal of Adolescent and Adult Literacy* 49, no. 1 (2005): 71–74.
Campbell, Patty. *Amazon.com* Review. 2005. www.amazon.com.
Dillon, Stacy, Jennifer Hubert, and Karyn Silverman. *Booklist*, 1 September 2007, 106.
Engberg, Gillian. *Booklist*, 1–15 January 2005, 852.
Frerichs, Joy. *ALAN Review* 33, no. 1 (2005): 42.
Haegele. Katie. *Philadelphia Inquirer*, 2005. www.thelalatheory.com/reviews.html.
Kirkus Reviews, 15 January 2005, 115.
Olson, Kristi. *Teenreads.com*, 2005. www.teenreads.com/reviews.
Publishers Weekly, 24 January 2005, 245.
Rohrlick, Paula. *Kliatt*, 1 March 2005.
Silverman, Karyn N. *School Library Journal* (February 2005): 132.
Stevenson, Deborah. *Bulletin of the Center for Children's Books* 58, no. 6 (2005).

Saudi Arabia

Shedd, Carol Johnson. *School Library Journal* (January 2001): 112.

Say Good-bye

Ralston, Jennifer. *School Library Journal* (July 2001): 102.

"Snake"

Campbell, Patty. *Amazon.com* Review. www.amazon.com.

Speak

Adams, Lauren. *Horn Book Magazine* 75, no. 5 (1999): 605–6.
Barr, Katherine. *ALAN Review* 27, no. 2 (2000).
Bulletin of the Center for Children's Books (October 1999): 45.
Carton, Debbie. *Booklist*, 15 September 1999, 247.
Hubert, Jennifer. *Amazon.com* Review. www.amazon.com.
Kirkus Reviews, 19 September 1999, 1496.
Library Journal (October 1999).
Mattson, Nancy. *CNN.com*, 29 November 1999. www.cnn.com.
Meacham, Maggie. *Children's Literature*, 2000. http://childrenslit.com.
New York Times Book Review, 12 March 2000.
Publishers Weekly, 13 September 1999, 85.
Ralston, Jennifer. *School Library Journal* 49, no. 10 (2003): 99.
Rohrlick, Paula. *Kliatt* (September 1999): 4.
Schwartz, Dana. *Teenreads.com*. www.teenreads.com/reviews.
Sherman, Dina. *School Library Journal* (October 1999): 144.
Smith, Sally. *Journal of Adolescent and Adult Literacy* 43, no. 6 (2000): 585–86.
Zvirin, Stephanie. *Booklist*, 15 November 2000, 632.

Thank You, Sarah: The Woman Who Saved Thanksgiving

Cooper, Ilene. *Booklist*, 15 December 2002, 764.
Kirkus Reviews, 1 October 2002, 1462.
Publishers Weekly, 23 September 2002, 26.
Sherman, Louise L. *School Library Journal* (December 2002): 116.

Turkey Pox

Courtot, Marilyn. *Children's Literature*, 2000. http://childrenslit.com.
DelNegro, Janice. *Bulletin of the Center for Children's Books* (November 1996): 89–90.
Devereaux, Elizabeth, and Diane Roback. *Publishers Weekly*, 30 September 1996, 87.
Gangemi, Lisa Marie, and Trevelyn E. Jones. *School Library Journal* (October 1996): 84.

Phelan, Carolyn. *Booklist*, 1 September 1996, 135.
Williams, Sharon White. *Childhood Education* (Winter 1997/1998).

Twisted

Adams, Lauren. *Horn Book Magazine* 83, no. 2 (2007): 191–92.
Burner, Joyce Adams. *School Library Journal* (Fall 2007).
Cary, Alice. *Teens Book Page*. www.bookpage.com/0703bp/children/twisted.html.
Coats, Karen. *Bulletin of the Center for Children's Books* 60, no. 8 (2007): 323.
Engberg, Gillian. *Booklist*, 1–15 January 2007, 78.
Farrey, Brian. *Teenreads.com*. www.teenreads.com/reviews.
Green, John. *New York Times Book Review*, 3 June 2007, 35.
Kaywell, Joan. *Journal of Adolescent and Adult Literacy* 51, no. 1 (2008): 76–77.
Kirkus Reviews, 15 February 2007, 167.
Marler, Myrna. *Kliatt*, 1 March 2007.
Publishers Weekly, 15 January 2007, 52–53.
Schirota, Erin. *School Library Journal* (May 2007): 128.

Wintergirls

Bolle, Sonja. *Newsday*, 9 April 2009.
Cardillo, Margaret. *Sun Sentinel*, 12 April 2009.
Corbett, Sue. *Miami Herald*, 28 March 2009.
Edwards, Carol A. *School Library Journal* (February 2009): 96.
Feinberg, Barbara. *New York Times Book Review*, 8 May 2009.
Kirkus Reviews, 1 February 2009: 154.
Kraus, Daniel. *Booklist*, 15 December 2008, 51.
Publishers Weekly, 26 January 2009, 120–21.
Stevenson, Deborah. *Bulletin of the Center for Children's Books* 62, no. 7 (2009).
Wood, Sarah W. *Teenreads.com*. www.teenreads.com/reviews.

Index

About the Author

Wendy J. Glenn is an associate professor in English education at the University of Connecticut. She received the 2009 University Teaching Fellow award and was named a Fulbright Scholar to Norway for the 2009–2010 academic year. As a scholar, Glenn explores questions related to young adult literature, writing, and culturally responsive pedagogies. She is the author of *Sarah Dessen: From Burritos to Box Office* and *Richard Peck: The Past Is Paramount* (with Don Gallo). She has published articles in *Research in the Teaching of English, ALAN Review, English Journal, Journal of Adolescent and Adult Literacy, English Leadership Quarterly, SIGNAL, Teacher Education Quarterly*, and *Thinking Classroom*. Glenn has served on the editorial review board of the *ALAN Review*, was an elected member of the ALAN Executive Board, and chaired the ALAN Amelia Elizabeth Walden Book Award committee. She has also served as editor for the Literary Analysis Section of the *Journal of Literacy Research* sponsored by the National Reading Conference.